GERMANY

Robert Gibson and Jon Nichol

GENERAL EDITOR **Jon Nichol**

Contents

Basil Blackwell

Introduction

What comes into your mind when you think of Germany? Look at **A**. What do these cartoon characters think about Germans? Now read **B**:

‘*Sir . . . I must say that I am heartily sick – living as a German married into English community – to be reminded at least twice a week through very biased films on television about the bad Nazis and nasty Germans in general. Funny that the German soldier always dies like a coward and a British or American under most heroic circumstances or through a vile attack by their enemy.*’ (**B**)

(letter to *The Times*, 16 November 1979)

What is the lady complaining about? Think about television series or films about Germany that you have seen. Then say what you think about **A** and **B**.

Germany has played an important part in twentieth century history. Germany itself has seen many changes from 1900–85. The maps at the back of this book show how its boundaries have changed.

In 1900 Germany was one of the most powerful countries in Europe (see pages 3–7). Germany was at the centre of the First World War, 1914–18 (see pages 8–9). After its defeat in the war, Germany got a new kind of government. The 'Weimar Republic', as it was called, had many problems (see pages 12–19). Few people supported the Republic and, although some of the problems seemed to be settled in the 1920s, an economic crisis of 1928–33 made possible the rise of Hitler's Nazi Party (see pages 14–21). Hitler and his party tried to change many aspects of life in Germany (see pages 22–39).

Hitler's foreign policy led to the Second World War, 1939–45 (see pages 38–41). Nazi leaders ordered the killing of millions of Jews and others (see pages 44–45). The war destroyed many German towns. For Germany the war ended in 1945, in defeat (see pages 48–49). Russia, America, Britain and France occupied Germany and tried to destroy Nazism (see pages 50–51).

As Russia and America, Britain and France found it difficult to work together, Germany was split into two. The future of the two Germanies lay outside the Germans' control (see pages 52–64).

A Part of a cartoon story 'Enemy at Bay'

This book aims to make you think about these changes, how and why they happened, and what effect they had on ordinary people.

The following titles have been widely used in the preparation of this book, and can provide more information on modern Germany:

Modern Germany V. R. Berghahn, Cambridge University Press 1982

Documents on Nazism Noakes and Pridham, Jonathan Cape 1974

1 Industry and People

What was it like to live in Germany around 1900?

Between 1890 and 1914 changes took place in Germany that affected many aspects of people's lives: where they lived; how they travelled; what jobs they did.

The German population was growing rapidly – from 41 million people in 1871 to 65 million in 1911. More people lived in towns (see **A**) and worked in industry (see **B**). The German economy was changing from one based on farming to one that relied on factories. We call this change an Industrial Revolution.

A Percentages of people in towns and villages

	More than 100 000 people	2000–100 000 people	Under 2000 people
1871	5%	31%	64%
1911	21%	39%	40%

B Percentages of people employed in agriculture and industry

Date	% in agriculture	% in industry
1871	50	30
1907	35	40

C Coal and steel output 1880–1913 (in tons)

Date	Coal output	
	GB	**Germany**
1880	150 million	45 million
1890	185 million	70 million
1900	230 million	110 million
1910	270 million	155 million
1913	290 million	190 million

Date	Steel output	
	GB	**Germany**
1880	1 million	1.5 million
1890	3.6 million	2.2 million
1900	4.9 million	6.3 million
1910	5.3 million*	10.9 million*
1913	6.9 million	18.6 million

*figures from 1908

D Changes in Germany 1890–1914

a Cheap grain was imported from the USA.
b There was a growth in the number of large factories.
c In 1881 Siemens had developed the world's first electrically-powered tram. Some German towns used trams.
d Daimler–Benz were developing the motor car. The use of motor cars spread.
e More people were going to university.

F Living conditions for poor Berliners in 1910

C shows how important the coal and steel industries had become by 1914. There were other changes too (see D).

The Industrial Revolution had its greatest impact in Berlin, central Germany and the Ruhr area. In some areas life was similar in 1914 to what it had been for hundreds of years; in other areas there was a strange mixture, as this German commented in 1909:

❝under ancient beams the most up-to-date machinery was installed and iron girders supported mud walls.❞ (**E**)

How did all these changes affect the German people? The following examples give an idea of what life in Germany was like for different people in 1900.

A Berlin factory worker He worked 10–12 hours a day, six days a week. He lived in a two-roomed flat like **F**.

His rent came to a quarter of his income, so he took in lodgers. He spent half his income on food, which was mostly bread. A doctor living in Berlin in 1890 commented:

❝the poverty of the big city opened up before my eyes, and the social causes of so many illnesses became all too apparent to me . . . healthy and strong people became ill because of the dust of the factory, the dark airless flats and the poor food, as well as the constant contact with illness . . . all you could do was to watch them die.❞ (G)

A self-employed craftsman A German writer described the life of a toymaker living in Germany in the 1870s:

❝The flats consist of two rooms . . . The workroom which also serves as a kitchen, where the children play and the craftsman works . . . and the other room in which there are two or three beds packed so closely together that you can't walk between them . . . at night at least two people sleep in each bed . . . the children have only one shirt . . . meals consist of potatoes . . . They (the craftsmen) sometimes work through the night to complete an order for delivery the next day . . . The last thing they want to do is to work in a factory.❞ (H)

A domestic servant J comes from a novel by Theodor Fontane. It tells us about the life of a maid with a wealthy family.

❝the sleeping quarters are always in the kitchen; right beside the stove or just opposite. You climb a ladder and if you're tired, you fall off. But mostly you make it, and then you open the door and push yourself in the opening, just like an oven . . . It's worst in summer . . . it's like being put on a spit.❞ (J)

A factory foreman A visitor to a factory in 1890 reported:

❝(the foreman's) very clothing distinguished them from others in the factory . . . they wore jacket, shirt and tie rather than overalls . . . they were the link between the workforce and the management . . .❞ (K)

L shows how they might have spent their spare time.

An engineer An observer commented on the work of an engineer in 1916:

❝The task of the scientific engineer is to build machines and run the factory with the least possible cost and the highest efficiency.❞ (M)

L Outside a country inn

P High-ranking military men and officials at a banquet

There was a shortage of engineers at this time, and those with a good technical education were well paid and respected.

A banker He had recently made money and had a house built. A visitor described the house:

❛*The banqueting hall, very vast and very lofty, and indeed the whole mansion, is built of every kind of rare marble, and where it is not marble it is gold.*❜ (**N**)

A landowner (*Junker*) He owned a large estate in East Prussia. He was used to wealth, produced grain and had owned a town house in Berlin. He had sold the Berlin house because he couldn't pay the rates. Together with the top people in the army and the civil service he was seen as one of the most important people in Germany. In 1938 a Prussian noble wrote about his past:

❛*fencing duels, drinking, jokes, hunting tales and the unending discoveries of friendships between individuals were the main themes of conversation.*❜ (**O**)

P shows where these conversations may have taken place.

??????????????????

1 Use the table below to say how each of these people would have reacted to the changes in. **D**. I or each, give a mark from 1–5, according to what the person might have thought about the change.
1 – strongly like; 2 – like; 3 – don't care; 4 – dislike; 5 – strongly dislike

Person	Change				
	a	b	c	d	e
Factory worker in Berlin					
Self-employed craftsman					
Banker					
Landowner (Junker)					

Give your reasons for each answer.

2 a Draw graphs to show the information in **A** and **C**.
b Use **C** to compare the coal and steel output of Germany and Great Britain, 1880–1913.

3 Use the evidence in this section to explain how and why life in Germany changed between 1890 and 1914. What other sorts of evidence might give us a fuller picture of these changes?

5

2 Politics and Foreign Policy

In 1871 Germany became a united country. It was formed from many different states. The most powerful of these was Prussia. Prussian kings became rulers of Germany. Wilhelm II (A), became *Kaiser* (Emperor) in 1888.

B shows how Germany was governed. The parliament, called the *Reichstag*, was elected by the people. Although the Reichstag could change laws, it was the Kaiser who had the power to introduce laws, select ministers, declare war and make peace. He once said that the members of the Reichstag were 'a troop of monkeys, a collection of blockheads and sleep-walkers'. There were different political parties within the Reichstag. C shows the main ones.

The Kaiser's main minister was the Chancellor. Between 1900 and 1917 the German Chancellors were Bülow (1900–9) and Bethmann Hollweg (1909–17).

The Kaiser and many Prussian civil servants, army officers and landowners, felt threatened by the changes that were happening in Germany (see page 3). They were also alarmed by the rise of the Social Democrats. In 1898 the Social Democrats had gained 56 seats in the Reichstag. By 1912 they had 110 seats, and were the largest party. Trade union membership was growing in

A Kaiser Wilhelm II

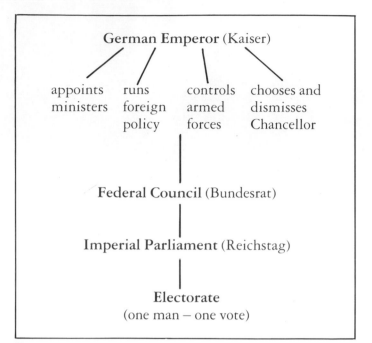

B The government system

Germany: in 1891 there had been 278 000 union members, by 1913 membership had risen to 2 549 000. This, too, worried the Kaiser.

For the Kaiser, the answer to these problems lay with foreign policy. If he had a popular foreign policy, he could gain the people's support. Bülow had realised this in 1897:

❛ *only a successful foreign policy can help to reconcile, pacify, rally, unite.* ❜ **(D)**

The main features of Germany's foreign policy from 1900–14 were:

Naval rivalry with Britain There was an enormous growth in the German navy between 1898 and 1914. A Navy League was founded and had a large number of supporters. Alfred von Tirpitz was one of the people responsible for the navy. He said to the Kaiser in 1897:

❛ *For Germany the most dangerous enemy at the present time is England . . . The military situation against England demands battleships in as great a number as possible.* ❜ **(E)**

Bethmann Hollweg described the reasons for building up the German navy and the effects it had:

❛ (The Kaiser's) *basic and primary idea is to destroy England's position in the world to the advantage of Germany; therefore – we need a navy and, to build it, a great deal of*

Party	Policies
Conservatives (various groups)	Many were more interested in agriculture than industry. Some disliked the growth of the navy and the search for colonies abroad.
Liberals	They supported the growth of industry, and wanted colonies to be established.
Centre Party	They were mainly Catholics. The Kaiser called them 'enemies of the Empire'.
Social Democrats	The workers' party: wanted better living conditions and shorter working hours. The Kaiser called them 'enemies of the Empire' and 'comrades without a country'.

C Main parties in the Reichstag

G Morocco

money; since only a wealthy country can provide it, Germany shall become wealthy; hence the encouragement given to industry and the anger of farmers, who protest against this policy to save themselves from ruin . . .* **(F)**

As the German Navy grew, so Britain increased the size of her fleet and introduced more powerful battleships like the *Dreadnought*.

'A place in the sun' The Kaiser wanted Germany to have a large overseas Empire. The years before 1914 saw Germany trying to increase its influence in all parts of the world.

Conflict with Russia Germany was building a railway link between Berlin and Baghdad. The Russians had their own plans for this area and were increasingly worried. Also, both Russia and Germany hoped to expand in the Balkans (see map inside back cover). By 1907 Russia was looking to Britain for an ally.

First Moroccan crisis In 1905 the French tried to increase their control over Morocco (see map **G**). The Germans hoped to weaken the growing friendship between Britain and France. With this in mind the Kaiser landed at Tangiers in March 1905 and made a speech supporting the independence of Morocco. At a conference at Algeciras in 1906 the French were allowed influence in Morocco. The crisis strengthened the friendship between Britain and France.

Balkan crisis In many Balkan states the people were demanding the right to run their own affairs. Austria–Hungary wanted to stop this, fearing that groups within the Austrian–Hungarian Empire would also demand independence. Russia also wanted to expand into the Balkans. In 1908 Austria–Hungary took over Bosnia. Germany supported this move. Germany also promised support if Austria–Hungary attacked Serbia and Russia declared war. Moltke, Chief of Staff of the German Army, wrote:

two mobilized armies like the German and French will not be able to stand side by side without resorting to war . . . Germany, when it mobilizes against Russia, must also reckon on a war with France. **(H)**

Second Moroccan crisis In 1911 the French sent troops to Fez (see map **G**). The Germans wanted to stop French influence in Morocco. They sent a gunboat, *Panther*, to Agadir. The British spoke out against this. The French and Germans made an agreement. Germany recognised French rights in Morocco, and the Germans gained some of the French Congo. The German navy withdrew from Agadir.

These crises had been solved without war. But tensions were increasing between the powers and within Germany, so that war soon seemed to be the only solution.

???????????????

1 Make a timechart for the events in this section. Include the following, and any others you consider to be important: Bosnian crisis; Social Democrats largest party in Reichstag; Agadir crisis; First Moroccan crisis.

2 Which political parties in **C** do you think each of the people on pages 3–5 would have supported? Why?

3 Imagine you are a British journalist living in Germany in 1912. Write a profile of the Kaiser for your newspaper. How might you expect your readers to feel about the Kaiser?

4 a Does **A** give a true picture of the Kaiser?
   b Why might Tirpitz wish to exaggerate the danger from Britain, in **E**?
   c How far is **F** based on fact?

3 The First World War

By 1907 Russia, France and Britain had agreed to help each other if attacked by Germany, Austria–Hungary or Italy. If war broke out, all six countries would fight. In Germany the Kaiser was worried by the success of the Social Democrats in the 1912 elections, and Germany's defeat in the Agadir crisis (see page 7). A successful war seemed to be a way of becoming popular again.

The Germans put large sums of money into building up the army. Army leaders wanted to fight before France and Russia had had time to develop their armies. Germany's Foreign Secretary later wrote down what he said to the German Chief of Staff, Moltke, on 20 May 1914:

❝If war appears inevitable, then one should not leave it to the enemy to dictate the moment, but choose it for oneself.❞ (A)

28 June	Assassination of Archduke Franz Ferdinand, heir to the Austrian throne, in Sarajevo.
28 July	Austria declared war on Serbia.
30 July	Russia mobilised troops in support of Serbia.
1 August	Germany declared war on Russia.
3 August	Germany declared war on France. Germany invaded Belgium.
4 August	Britain declared war on Germany.

B The steps to war

To get the support of the whole country the war had to appear necessary for the defence of Germany. **B** shows the steps to war. The final 'moment' came in the summer of 1914. Admiral von Müller wrote in his diary on 1 August 1914:

❝The mood is brilliant. The government has managed magnificently to appear the attacked party.❞ (C)

The First World War had begun.

On 25 July the Social Democrats' leaders said that Austria 'wasn't worth a drop of German blood'. **D** shows a different reaction. A new recruit commented, 'war is like Christmas', and a novelist recorded 'at last life regained an ideal significance . . . the war would cleanse mankind from all its impurities'. By 4 August the Social Democrats had changed their minds. They voted in the Reichstag for money to be made available for fighting the war. The country at last seemed to be united, and the Kaiser announced 'I no longer recognise parties: I recognise only Germans.'

D Many Germans welcomed the outbreak of war

E German soldiers in the trenches on the Western Front

The Western Front	
1914	*6–9 September* Battle of Marne. France halts German advance.
1915	*April–May* Battle of Ypres. Minor gains for Germany.
1916	*February–November* Struggle for Verdun. German success at first. *June–November* Battle of Somme.
1917	*February–March* Germans retreat to Siegfried Line. *April* USA joins Allies to fight against Germany.
1918	*Spring* German offensive beaten back.

The Eastern Front	
1914	*August* Battle of Tannenberg – German victory. *September* Battle of Masurian Lakes – German victory.
1914–15	Russian advance into Hungary stopped.
1915	Germans advance into Russia.
1916	*June–August* Russian offensive.
1917	*December* Armistice.
1918	*March* Treaty of Brest–Litovsk between Russia and Germany.

F Main campaigns of the First World War

The Germans decided to follow the *Schlieffen Plan*, drawn up by General Schlieffen in 1905–6. His aim was to avoid war against Russia and France at the same time. So the plan was to attack France through Belgium, and then concentrate on defeating Russia. But things didn't go according to plan.

German troops crossed the Belgian frontier and advanced into France to the River Marne. Britain had promised to protect Belgium against foreign invasion, and French and British troops stopped a further German advance. Stalemate had been reached. Four years of trench warfare followed. E shows a trench on the Western Front in 1914. The use of machine guns, poison gas and heavy artillery meant that hundreds of thousands of soldiers died.

Meanwhile the Russians invaded East Prussia, but were defeated by the Germans under Generals Hindenburg and Ludendorff. In 1915 the Germans made an advance into Russia. The Russians led an offensive in 1916, but withdrew from the war in 1917 when the Communists came to power.

F shows the main campaigns of the First World War. You can read more about what happened in *The First World War* in this series.

The Home Front

Inside Germany people soon faced severe shortages of food. There were bad harvests, and the British mounted a *blockade* of German ports (surrounded them to cut off supplies). The German Navy did little to stop the blockade.

Later, a Berliner wrote in his autobiography:

((In 1916) *a general war weariness became apparent . . . the great broad mass of people vegetated into sullen lethargy. The queues at the food shops grew longer every day. In the queues were thin faces, weak bodies and hungry eyes. People watched the others to make sure that they were not getting more than anyone else. What had once . . . been a popular movement now seemed to be destroyed . . . Nobody read the posters and the reports from the front any more. Grumbling spread. Demonstrations for food turned into ones for peace. Victory or defeat, heroism, battles, the Kaiser's speeches . . . it suddenly all became unimportant . . . hunger penetrated a little into the rich districts . . . hunger was a ghost, invisible but to be felt everywhere.*) (G)

The Centre Party, Liberals and Social Democrats thought that the war should only continue if it was to defend Germany. They passed a resolution for peace in 1917. After the failure of the spring offensive in 1918 the Germany Army retreated. The Armistice in the West was signed on 11 November 1918. For some people Germany's war had caused more problems than it had solved, as H shows.

H Effects of the War on Germany

a 2.4 million Germans were killed.
b 70% of the cost of the war had been met by loans. People had been sure that Germany would win and get the money back.
c Prices rose rapidly.
d The army under Hindenburg and Ludendorff had taken power over civilian life as well as the running of the war.
e The gap between the rich and poor in Germany increased.

??????????????

1 a Why did many Germans want war in 1914?
b Why did Social Democrats change their attitude to war between July and August 1914?
c Why, according to the writer of **G**, did many people want peace by 1916? Can we trust what he says?

2 Imagine you are one of the people in **D**. You have been sent to the Western Front (**E**). Write a diary entry for one day, describing life in the trenches. Did you expect war to be like this?

3 Compare the Kaiser's position in 1914 and in summer 1918. How had it changed? How would you account for the changes?

4 Why was Germany defeated in the First World War?

4 Germany 1918-19

November 1918. The First World War had ended, and Germany's ruler, the Kaiser, had fled to Holland. The country was in chaos, and many people went short of food. In Kiel, workers and sailors set up a council like a Russian soviet to run the city. Soon soldiers and workers did the same in many other German cities, like Hamburg and Munich. A German soldier wrote down his memories of the end of the First World War:

❛ *In November the general tension increased. Then one day the disaster came upon us, suddenly and without warning. Sailors arrived in lorries and called on all to revolt, a few Jewish youths being the leaders in that struggle for the "freedom, beauty and dignity of our national life". Not one of them had been to the front. The rumours grew more and more definite. What I had imagined to be a local affair was apparently a general revolution. In addition to all this, distressing news came back from the front. They wanted to surrender. Yes – was such a thing possible? In vain all the sacrifices and suffering, in vain the starvation and thirst for many endless months, in vain the hours we spent doing our duty, gripped by fear of death, and in vain the death of two millions of men! At the end of November 1918 I returned to Munich. I rejoined the reserve battalion of my regiment, which was in the hands of the 'Soldiers' Councils'.* ❜ **(A)**

The soldier was Adolf Hitler, later ruler of Germany.

For a time it seemed that Germany might follow the Communist path that Russia had taken in November 1917. But this did not happen. On 9 November 1918 the leaders of the largest political party, the Social Democrats, declared that the country was now a *republic*. They took over Germany's government until a new plan could be worked out for governing the country. In January 1919 electors chose a National Assembly. For the first time everyone over 20 had the vote. At the same time, the *Spartacists* (a group of Communists) seized the main government buildings in Berlin, and tried to set up their own government. A poet living in Berlin wrote:

❛ Monday, 13 January 1919 *At twenty to eleven at night there was an outbreak of violent fighting, with rifle fire and the pounding and chatter of heavy and light machine-guns. It seemed right outside my door. Sometimes it sounded as though the door was being stove in by rifle-butts . . . The Spartacists, their major effort having failed, are conducting a guerilla war, by day from the roof-tops, by night from out-of-the-way streets. Liebknecht (the Spartacist leader) has disappeared.* ❜ **(B)**

Friedrich Ebert, the Social Democrat leader, asked the army and the *Freikorps* (bands of ex-soldiers) for help against the Communists **(C)**. The army and Freikorps

C Barricades in the streets of Berlin during the Spartacist Uprising

E Children round a street soup kitchen, December 1918

put down the Spartacists, and murdered their leaders, Karl Liebnecht and Rosa Luxemburg.

Friedrich Lennhoff was a 15-year-old schoolboy in 1918. His Jewish father owned a factory in Berlin. **D** is what Friedrich wrote in his autobiography about life in Berlin from November 1918 to February 1919:

❛*When the Kaiser fled to Holland, the front lines had cracked, the soldiers retreated in disarray, and they were in a state of shock. The streets were full of lorries with sailors, soldiers and workers brandishing red flags, and there was fighting and gunfire in the streets around my home, which was itself damaged in many places. Electricity had been cut off and the factory was virtually at a standstill. The house was lit by a single gas lamp . . . the family kept close together, often afraid to venture out in fear of stray bullets. Amidst all this turmoil mother suggested to me that I should start to keep a diary, which I did, combining it with a scrapbook to help me sort out my . . . feelings about the past, present and future.* ❜
(D)

Although Friedrich's family was well-off, he might have seen other children like the ones in **E**.

?????????????????

1 a Who were: the Spartacists; the Freikorps?
b Why did Hitler think the 'sacrifices and sufferings' were in vain (**A**)?
c Why did the men in the lorries wave red flags (**D**)?
d Who was Liebknecht, and what happened to him?
e Why do you think the children in **E** were queueing for food?

2 Imagine you are a young person living in Berlin from November 1918 to February 1919. Make up a diary or scrapbook account of events there. You should include: the flight of the Kaiser and the end of the war; street fighting during the Spartacist rising; life at home.

3 Look at **A**, **B**, **C**, and **D**. Are any of them *biased* (one-sided)? If so, how?

4 What problems faced the German Republic from 1918–19? How did it attempt to deal with them? How successful were these attempts?

5 Weimar and Versailles

The National Assembly met in February 1919. Two months later, in April, a Communist revolution took place in Munich, Bavaria. Again the army and Freikorps crushed the revolt. Among them was an army corporal, Adolf Hitler.

Because of street fighting in Berlin, the National Assembly met in the small and peaceful town of Weimar. This town gave its name to the plan or *constitution* which the National Assembly worked out for ruling the country. On 31 July 1919 the National Assembly accepted the new constitution.

The Weimar Republic was a democracy. That is, all voters over 20 elected members for the two houses of Parliament, and chose a president. For the first time all the workers in the Lennhoffs' Berlin factory (see page 11) had the vote. The electorate chose an upper house or *Reichsrat* to represent each of Germany's individual states. The lower house, or *Reichstag*, represented all Germany. The lower house was the more important, and the government ministers were chosen from its members. The number of MPs a party had depended on how many people voted for it. This system is called *proportional representation*. It meant that there was a large number of parties. Table **A** shows the four most important parties in January 1919.

Elections for the two houses of parliament were held every four years, and presidential elections every seven. The president commanded the army, and had the power to dissolve the Reichstag and call new elections. These powers played a big part in the events which led to the rise of Hitler.

Friedrich Ebert was the first president of the Weimar Republic. In its first four years, the Republic had nine *coalition* governments (governments made up from different parties). They faced serious problems. The German economic crisis continued, with inflation (rising cost of living), high unemployment, and widespread hunger.

In June 1919 the Weimar Republic received a major blow when it had to accept the Versailles Settlement – the peace treaty drawn up by the powers which had won the war. The Versailles Treaty dominated Germany's history from 1919–41. Some of its terms suggest why:

❛42 *Germany is forbidden to maintain or construct any fortification either on the left bank of the Rhine, or on the right bank to the west of a line drawn 50 km to the east.*

45 *As compensation for the destruction of the coal mines in the north of France, and as part payment towards the total reparations due, Germany gives to France the coal mines of the Saar.*

49 *Germany hands over to the League of Nations, as trustees, the government of the Saar. At the end of 15 years, its inhabitants shall be asked under which government they wish to be placed.*

80 *Germany respects the independence of Austria.*

87 *Germany respects the complete independence of Poland.*

89 *Poland agrees to allow free passage of persons, goods and mails between East Prussia and the rest of Germany.*

102 *The Allied powers agree to set up the town of Danzig as a free city. It will be placed under the protection of the League of Nations.*

103 *Germany renounces all her rights and claims over her overseas possessions.*

160 *By a date not later than March 31, 1920, the German Army must not consist of more than 7 divisions of infantry and 3 of cavalry. After that date the total number of effectives in the Army of . . . Germany must not exceed one hundred thousand men.*

231 *The Allied governments affirm, and Germany accepts, the responsibility of Germany and her allies for causing all the loss and damage to which the Allied governments and their peoples have been subjected as a result of the war.*

232 *The Allied governments recognise that the resources of Germany are not adequate to make complete reparation for such loss and damage . . . But they require, and Germany undertakes, that she will make compensation for all the damage done to the civilian population of the Allied Powers and to their property during the war.*

233 *The amount of the above damage shall be determined by an interallied commission.*

A Main parties in the National Assembly, 1919

Name	Nature	Votes	Seats
Social Democratic Party	Socialist	11 509 000	165
Centre Party	Conservative, Catholic	5 980 000	91
National People's Party	Right-wing, Nationalist	(not known)	44
German Democratic Party	Left-wing, Liberal	5 642 000	75

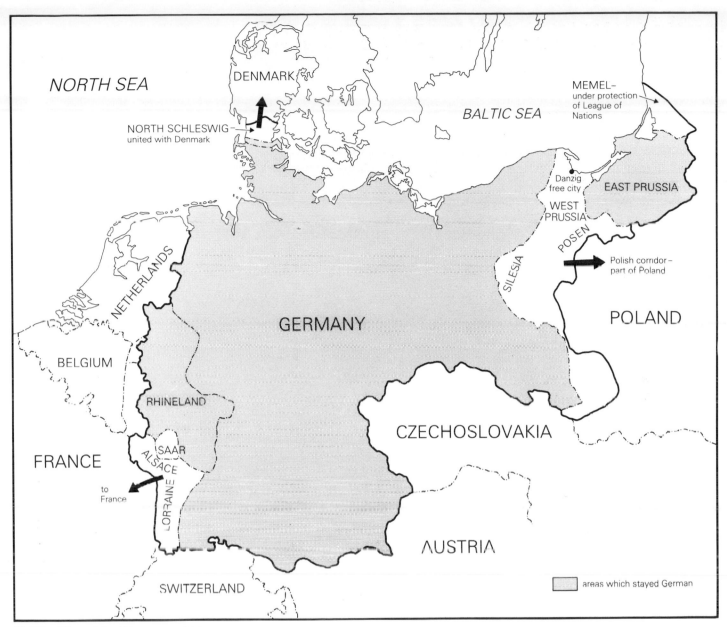

C The Versailles Treaty and Germany

Labels on map:
NORTH SEA
DENMARK
NORTH SCHLESWIG — united with Denmark
BALTIC SEA
MEMEL — under protection of League of Nations
Danzig free city
EAST PRUSSIA
WEST PRUSSIA
POSEN
SILESIA
Polish corridor — part of Poland
NETHERLANDS
GERMANY
POLAND
BELGIUM
RHINELAND
CZECHOSLOVAKIA
FRANCE
SAAR
ALSACE
LORRAINE
to France
AUSTRIA
SWITZERLAND
areas which stayed German

428 *As a guarantee that the Treaty shall be carried out, the German territory to the west of the Rhine will be occupied by . . . Allied troops for 15 years.* ❯ **(B)**

Many ex-soldiers and sailors joined extreme groups who refused to accept Versailles. They called the Weimar politicians traitors for signing and accepting the Versailles Treaty. In March 1920 an armed force consisting mainly of ex-soldiers and their officers rebelled and seized government buildings in Berlin. Ebert's government seemed powerless. The army refused to fight old comrades. This rising, the *Kapp Putsch* (named after one of its leaders) failed only because of a general strike of workers in Berlin.

??????????????????

1 Map **C** shows some of the effects of the peace treaties drawn up at the end of the First World War. Copy the map. Now look carefully at the terms of the Versailles Settlement (**B**). Make short notes on the terms, and add them to the map.

2 a Why did many Germans hate the Versailles Settlement?
b How did some of them react to it in 1920?
c What kinds of evidence might help an historian understand how the Germans felt about Versailles? (newspaper reports, letters . . .)

13

6 Origins of the Nazi Party

B Hitler addressing an early session of the German Workers' Party

In September 1919 the army ordered Hitler to keep an eye on small extremist groups. He attended a gathering of some 20 members of the German Workers' Party. To his surprise, they asked him to come to a meeting of the party's committee on the following Wednesday. Hitler wrote:

Wednesday came. The tavern in which the meeting was to take place was a very run down place . . . In the dim light of a broken down gas lamp, four young people sat at a table . . . They at once greeted me joyfully . . . The minutes of the last meeting were read . . . Next came the treasurer's report – all in all, the association possessed seven marks and fifty pfennigs . . . Terrible, terrible. I now began to question – but aside from a few directives, there was nothing, no programmes, no leaflets, no printed matter at all, no membership cards, not even a miserable rubber stamp, only obvious good faith and good intentions. (A)

Hitler joined and took over the party. Soon he was organising its members and meetings, and working out its programme. **B** is a later painting of one of these party sessions. **C** is Hitler's account of an early meeting.

The meeting was to be opened at 7.30. At 7.15 I entered the hall of the Hofbräuhaus in Munich, and my heart nearly burst for joy. The gigantic hall was overcrowded with people, shoulder to shoulder, numbering almost two thousand. And above all – those people to whom we wanted to appeal had come. For more than half the hall seemed to be occupied by communists and socialists. They had resolved that our first demonstration would come to a speedy end.

But it turned out differently. After the first speaker had finished, I took the floor. A few minutes later there was a hail of shouts, there were violent clashes in the hall, a handful of the most faithful war comrades and other supporters battled with the disturbers, and only little by little were able to restore order. I was able to proceed. Half an hour later the applause began to drown the interruptions and hooting, and finally, when I had taken up the programme and began to explain the 25 points for the first time, I had before me a hall full of people united in a new conviction, a new faith, a new will. (C)

In 1920 the German Workers' Party became the National German Workers' Party (the Nazi Party). **D** shows some of the '25 points' in the Nazi programme.

Hitler was a great *orator* (speech-maker). At public meetings he swayed many people to support the Nazis. The Nazis' enemies, particularly the Communists, often attacked them violently. To fight their opponents, the Nazis founded their own private army – the *Sturmabteilung* (storm-troopers) or SA. Hitler wrote:

❮*As early as the summer of 1920 the troops for keeping order were gradually taking definite form, and by the spring of 1921 they were divided in time into companies, which again were divided into smaller sections. This had become urgently necessary, since in the meantime our activities as regards meetings had been increasing continuously.*❯ (E)

On 4 November 1921 Hitler was due to speak at a rally in the Circus Krone, Munich. His account (**F**) tells us how the SA got their name. The meeting had just begun when:

❮*In a few seconds the hall was filled with a yelling and howling mob, above which numberless pint pots flew like howitzer shells. Chair legs smashed, glasses shivered; howls and screams. It was a mad spectacle . . . The trouble had hardly begun when my storm-troopers, as they were named from that day forth, attacked. Like wolves they rushed again and*

again in parties of eight or ten on the enemy, and began gradually to sweep them out of the hall. After five minutes I could see hardly one who was not streaming with blood. For twenty minutes the hellish row lasted, but then our enemies, who must have numbered 700–800 men, had for the most part been beaten out of the hall . . . by my men numbering not even 50 . . .❯ (F)

Photograph **G** shows demonstrating SA men carrying a banner announcing 'Death to Marxism'.

G SA men in an anti-Communist parade

D Extracts from the Nazi Party's programme

1 We demand the union of all Germans . . . to form a Great Germany.

2 We demand equality of rights for the German People in its dealings with other nations, and the abolition of the Peace Treaty of Versailles.

3 We demand land and territory for the nourishment of our people and for settling our surplus population.

4 None but members of the nation may be members of the State. None but those of German blood . . . may be members of the nation. No Jew, therefore, may be a member of the nation.

6 The right of voting is to be enjoyed by citizens of the State alone . . . all official appointments shall be granted to citizens of the state alone.

8 All further non-German immigration must be prevented.

11 We demand the abolition of incomes unearned by work.

14 We demand that there shall be profit-sharing in the great industries.

15 We demand a generous development of provision for old age.

17 We demand . . . the passing of a law for the confiscation without compensation of land for communal purposes . . . and prohibition of all speculation in land.

18 We demand ruthless war against all whose activities injure the common interest. Common criminals against the nation – money lenders, profiteers etc – must be punished with death.

19 We demand the education of specially gifted children of poor parents at the expense of the State.

?????????????????

1 a What did Hitler think was wrong with the German Workers' Party when he joined it?
b What methods did he use to build up the Nazi Party?

2 Look at **D**. What was Nazi policy on: Austria; the Versailles Settlement; land; Jews; industry; education?

3 Write an account of the meeting in **F** from the viewpoint of a Communist who was there. How do the accounts differ?

4 a What impression of Hitler is the artist of **B** trying to give?
b Which piece of evidence, **A** or **B**, tells us more about Hitler's meetings?
c In what ways might **F** and **G** be biased?

7 The Great Inflation

January 1919	8.9
January 1920	64.8
January 1921	64.9
January 1922	191.8
January 1923	17 972
July	353 412
August	4 620 455
September	98 860 000
October	25 260 208 000
November 15	4 200 000 000 000

A The falling value of the Mark, 1919–23
(equivalent in Mark of 1 American dollar)

	1914	1918	1922	August 1923	November 1923
1 egg	0.08	0.25	180	5000	80 000 000
500g meat	0.9	2	1200	90 000	3 200 000 000
500g butter	1.4	3	2400	150 000	6 000 000 000
1kg bread	0.32	0.53	163	69 000	201 000 000
500g potatoes	0.04	0.12	80	2000	50 000 000

B Food prices 1914–23 (in Reichsmark)

C One million Marks

A shows what happened to the value of the German *Mark* between 1914 and 1923. **B** shows what effect this had on the cost of living in Germany.

Why did the Mark become worthless? Historians still argue about this question, but most have found the roots of the problem in the First World War. The war cost the German government a great deal of money. They borrowed money from industry, banks and ordinary people. This seemed a safe enough thing to do as they were sure that they could win the war, and make other countries pay the bill. But Germany lost. Far from being able to ask others for money, Germany had to pay damages to the Allies. These payments were demanded from Germany in the Treaty of Versailles and were called *reparations*. The Allies fixed the amount of reparations in April 1921 at 132 000 million gold marks to be paid over 66 years. One way that the new German government tried to pay its debts and the reparations was by printing more banknotes (**C**). Some foreigners were not impressed:

❝*Germany is teeming with wealth. She is humming like a beehive. The comfort and prosperity of her people absolutely astound me. Poverty is practically non-existent . . . And yet*

this is a country that is determined that she will not pay her debts . . . They are a nation of actors . . . If it wasn't for the fact that the Germans are guiltless of humour, one might imagine the whole nation was bent on perpetrating an elaborately laborious practical joke . . . ❞ (**D**)

(*The Times*, 18 April 1922)

By December 1922 the German government had stopped reparation payments. The French decided to go and get their money. In January 1923 French troops invaded Germany's most important coal-mining and industrial area, the Ruhr (see map inside front cover). The German government ordered workers and officials not to co-operate with the French. This policy of 'passive resistance' cost the German government money. Now Germany had to import coal from abroad, and support the workers who were resisting the French. The government's income fell and its expenditure rose. The German government printed even more banknotes. By 1923 German inflation was at its height. Egon Larsen later commented on the events.

❝*Bartering became more and more widespread . . . A haircut cost a couple of eggs . . . A student I knew . . . had sold his gallery ticket . . . at the State Opera for one dollar to an American; he could live on that money quite well for a whole week. The most dramatic changes in Berlin's outward appearance were the masses of beggars in the streets . . . The hard core of the street markets were the petty black-marketeers . . . In the summer of that inflation year my grandmother found herself unable to cope. So she asked one of her sons to sell her house. He did so for I don't know how many thousands of millions of marks. The old woman decided to keep the money under her mattress and buy food with it as the need arose — with the result that nothing was left except a pile of worthless paper when she died a few months later.*

As soon as the factory gates opened and the workers streamed out, pay packets (often in old cigar boxes) in their hands, a kind of relay race began: the wives grabbed the money, rushed to the nearest shops, and bought food before prices went up again. Salaries always lagged behind, the employees on monthly pay were worse off than workers on weekly. People living on fixed incomes sank into deeper and deeper poverty.

A familiar sight in the streets were handcarts and laundry baskets full of paper money, being pushed or carried to or from the banks. It sometimes happened that thieves stole the baskets but tipped out the money and left it on the spot. There was a dry joke that spread through Germany: papering one's WC with banknotes. Some people made kites for their kids out of them. ❯ (E)

Erna von Pustau remembered life in Hamburg at this time:

❮ We were deceived, too. We used to say, "All of Germany is suffering from inflation." It was not true. There is no game in the whole world in which everyone loses. Someone has to be the winner. The winners in our inflation were big business men in the cities and the "Green Front"; from peasants to the Junkers, in the country. The great losers were the working class and above all the middle class, who had most to lose.

How did big business win? Well, from the very beginning they figured their prices in gold value, selling their goods at gold value prices and paying their workers in inflated marks.

. . . You could go to the baker in the morning and buy two rolls for 20 marks; but go there in the afternoon, and the same rolls were 25 marks. The baker didn't know how it happened that the rolls were more expensive in the afternoon. His customers didn't know how it happened. It had somehow to do with the dollar, somehow to do with the stock exchange – and somehow, maybe to do with the Jews.

H The Reichsbank, Berlin, in 1923

Shoe factories paid their workers in bonds for shoes which they could exchange at the bakery for bread or the meat market for meat. ❯ (F)

The American writer Ernest Hemingway, working for the *Toronto Daily Star*, made a visit to a German town on the border with France:

❮ The French cannot come over to buy up all the cheap goods they would like to. But they can come over and eat . . . This miracle of exchange makes a swinish spectacle where the youth of the town of Strasbourg crowd into the German pastry shop to eat themselves sick, and gorge on fluffy, cream – filled slices of German cake at five marks the slice. The contents of the pastry shop are swept clear in half an hour . . . ❯ (G)

H shows messengers at the Reichsbank.

?????????????????

1 Fill in the table below to show who lost and who gained from inflation. Use the evidence in this section to help you and give reasons for each answer. One is done for you as an example.

Person	Gain	Stay same	Loss	Reason
	+	0	—	
Student				
American tourist	+			He had dollars
Street trader				
Pensioner				
Factory worker				
Office worker				
Businessman				
Peasant				
Landowner (Junker)				
French tourist				

2 a Why has the banknote **C** been overprinted?
  b What might be in the baskets in **H**, and why?
  c What do **A** and **B** tell us about German inflation?

3 Explain the meaning of the sentences in **E**, **F** and **G** which have been underlined. Why should the historian approach sources like these with special care?

4 What caused the German inflation of 1923? What effects did it have?

8 The Crisis of Weimar 1923

Many German people blamed the government for inflation. In the summer of 1923 many workers went on strike. Chancellor Cuno resigned, and was replaced by Gustav Stresemann. Stresemann ordered the workers in the Ruhr to end their 'passive resistance' (see page 16) and to go back to work. Nationalists, Nazis and Communists, who usually disagreed with each other, now united in opposition to Stresemann. Some army leaders made plans for a takeover.

Stalin, who was later to be leader of Russia, thought that there would be a revolution in Germany:

❝The German Revolution will be more important than the Russian Revolution, and the centre of World Revolution will move from Moscow to Berlin.❞ (A)

The Weimar Republic was threatened from all sides. Chart **B** shows the main events of 1923.

January	French and Belgian troops invaded Ruhr. 'Passive resistance' ordered by Chancellor Cuno (see page 16).
August	Stresemann became Chancellor. 'Passive resistance' ended.
October	Socialist governments in Saxony and Thuringia.
November	Hitler Putsch in Munich. Currency reform.

B Timechart: January – November 1923

Hitler wanted to make use of the weakness of the government, and to take over power. Hitler's Nazi Party joined with other groups who were against the Republic to form the *Kampfbund*. They planned a march on Berlin using the excuse that the left-wing (Socialist and Communist) governments of Saxony and Thuringia needed to be crushed. Stresemann acted before this could happen, and ordered the removal of Communist ministers from Saxony and Thuringia.

Gustav von Kahr was in charge of security in Bavaria, and had supported Hitler's Kampfbund. Kahr now dropped out of the plan for a march on Berlin. Hitler was determined to go ahead. Hitler now needed a situation where he could force Kahr to join him. The chance came on 8 November 1923 when Kahr was to speak at a meeting in a Munich beer cellar. General von Lossow (army commander), Colonel von Seisser (police leader), and other important Bavarian politicians were to be there. Hitler posted 600 SA men outside the meeting hall. Then he burst in and interrupted Kahr's speech.

An eye-witness wrote:

❝ . . . there was a movement at the entrance as if people were wanting to push their way in . . . Eventually steel helmets came into sight . . . People stood on chairs so that I didn't see Hitler until he had come fairly near along the main gangway; just before he turned to the platform, I saw him emerge between two armed soldiers in steel helmets who carried pistols next to their heads, pointing at the ceiling. They turned towards the platform, Hitler climbed on to a chair on my left. The hall was restless, and then Hitler made a sign to the man on his right, who fired a shot at the ceiling. Thereupon Hitler called out (I cannot recall the exact order of his words): 'The national revolution has broken out. The hall is surrounded.' He asked the gentlemen Kahr, Lossow, Seisser to come out . . . everything would be over in ten minutes if the gentlemen would go out with him. To my surprise the three gentlemen went out with him immediately . . .❞ (C)

Hitler offered the three men positions in a new government.

According to an account prepared by the Bavarian police Hitler had told the men:

❝Everybody must take up the post which he is allotted. . . . You must fight with me, achieve victory with me, or die with me. If things go wrong, I have four bullets in my pistol, three for my colleagues if they desert me, the last bullet for myself.❞ (D)

After much persuasion the three men reluctantly agreed to support Hitler. An hour after Hitler's first appearance they all returned into the hall. By this time the First World War veteran, Ludendorff, had turned up.

On the next day (9 November) it was clear that the army would not support Hitler, despite the fact that Hitler's supporters had taken over the army headquarters in Munich. Kahr also now refused to agree to support the *putsch* (armed uprising). Hitler's last hope was that a mass demonstration of support in the centre of Munich would persuade Kahr and the others to go along with him. Egon Larsen was there:

❝It was nine o'clock when I arrived on the Marienplatz, the central square of the inner town. There was a huge mass of citizens, with a couple of tramcars stuck in their midst. A man stood on an open car, speaking . . . Someone in the crowd told me that the speaker was Julius Streicher . . . a year ago he had joined the Hitler party with a little ultra-nationalist society he had founded. . . . At my bank the shutters were

F Julius Streicher addressing the crowds on the Marienplatz

down. The caretaker told me that the manager — it was a Jewish-owned firm — had decided to close shop and send the staff home. So I walked back, past the many fresh posters I had not yet seen: "Proclamation to the German People! The Berlin government of the November criminals has today been declared deposed. A new provisional national government has been formed. It consists of General Ludendorff, Adolf Hitler, General von Lossow and Colonel von Seisser . . ." In the distance machine guns started their rattattatt . . . **(E)**

Photograph **F** shows the scene that Larsen described.

Hitler's putsch ended when the police opened fire and 16 of Hitler's supporters were killed. Hitler was arrested. At his trial he said to the judges:

You may pronounce us guilty a thousand times, but the Goddess who presides over the Eternal Court of History will with a smile tear in pieces the charge of the Public Prosecutor and the verdict of this court. For she acquits us. **(G)**

Hitler was sentenced to five years imprisonment, but was let out after nine months.

?????????????????

1 a Why did the following groups oppose the government in 1923: workers; Nationalists; Nazis; Communists; the army?
b What action did these groups take?
c How did the Weimar Republic manage to survive the threats from the Kampfbund and Hitler?

2 Political parties are often described as 'Right-wing' or 'Left-wing'. Place the following on a scale from Left to Right: Stresemann; German Army; Communists; Kahr; Hitler; Social Democrats.

3 Which phrases in **C** show that the writer is not sure of what he says? How reliable is his account?

4 Imagine you are one of the people in photograph **F**. Write about what you see and hear. Use the evidence in this section to make up conversations you might have heard in the crowd, about the events of 8 November and Streicher's speech.

19

9 The 'Golden Twenties'

Foreign Policy

For a brief period in 1923 Gustav Stresemann was Chancellor. He then became Foreign Minister. The crisis of 1923 had shown that Germany could not pay all the reparations that the Allies demanded. Stresemann asked for a cut in reparations. In 1924 an American banker, Charles Dawes, led an international commission to look into the problem. The resulting *Dawes Plan* said that the French occupation of the Ruhr was to end. In return, Germany had to agree to pay reparations each year. The Allies would lend money to Germany so that its industry could get going again.

Some people in Germany did not like the idea of relying on loans from America. General Ludendorff shouted in the Reichstag:

This is a disgrace to Germany. Ten years ago I won the battle of Tannenberg. Today you have made a Jewish Tannenberg. (A)

In 1925 Stresemann negotiated the Treaty of Locarno with the Allies. Germany had to accept the western frontiers laid down in the Treaty of Versailles. Germany recognised that it was not allowed to put troops into the Rhineland (it was to be *demilitarised*).

In a letter of 7 September 1925 Stresemann defined his aims in foreign policy:

I think there are three great tasks which confront German foreign policy in the more immediate future.

In the first place the solving of the Reparations question in a sense acceptable for Germany, and the securing of peace which must underlie the recovery of our strength.

Secondly, the protection of Germans abroad, those 10 to 12 million of our people who now live under a foreign yoke in foreign lands.

The third great task is to change our eastern frontiers; recover Danzig, the Polish corridor and alter the frontier in Upper Silesia.

In the background stands the union with Austria. (B)

Army leaders drew up another list of aims in 1926:

1 The liberation of the Rhineland and Saar area.
2 The abolition of the Corridor and the regaining of Polish Upper Silesia.
3 The Anschluss of (union with) German Austria.
4 The abolition of the Demilitarised Zone. (C)

(Stülpnagel to the German Foreign Office, 6 March 1926)

In 1926 Stresemann got Germany into the League of Nations. In November of that year British forces left the Rhineland. The *Kellogg Pact* of 1928 was an international agreement which Germany supported, saying that war was not the right way to solve disputes between countries.

At another conference in 1929 a committee led by an American, Owen Young, suggested that reparations be reduced, and a date fixed when they should end. The date was to be 1988. Stresemann accepted the *Young Plan*. In June 1930 the French finally left the Rhineland.

Industry and People

On 15 November 1923 the German government began to reform the currency. It changed Germany's money in order to stop inflation. The banks recalled the old notes and issued new ones. They called the new currency the *Rentenmark*. People began to trust money again, especially when they saw industry recovering (see **D**).

After 1924 there was an increase in the demand for goods. New machines were installed in factories to replace those taken away as part of reparation payments. The economy was helped by loans from abroad. By 1927 Germany's economy was at last on the same level as it had been in 1913.

D Production in key German industries 1913–25

Year	Coal	Iron	Steel
1913	100	100	100
1915	77.2	61.1	69.8
1920	69.1	33.1	48.5
1923	32.8	25.6	36
1925	69.8	52.7	69.8

E How life in Germany changed

1 The eight-hour working day was brought in.
2 All workers would get the dole if they lost their jobs.
3 Firms gave their workers a say in decision-making.
4 On average, people lived longer.
5 By the end of the 1920s people were buying as many luxury goods as they had in 1913.
6 Private ownership of cars increased:

1914	60 800
1922	82 700
1925	175 600
1927	268 000
1930	501 200

7 The income of skilled workers and businessmen grew more quickly than that of clerks and unskilled workers. The income of farmers remained well below the average.
8 The government set up schemes to build new houses.

G Part of a painting by the German artist Otto Dix, showing fashionable life in Berlin in the 1920s

How did all this affect people in Germany? E is a list of changes in Germany in the 1920s.

Cultural life flourished. A German poet living in Berlin in the 1920s commented:

❝ *Theatres, opera and concert houses were filled to capacity. European artists from Paris, London, and Rome who came to Berlin were excited by it and didn't want to leave. The atmosphere in Berlin was electric.* ❞ (**F**)

G is an artist's impression of this time.

Politics

H shows the performance of some parties in the Reichstag elections. As no single party had a majority in the Reichstag, coalitions had to be formed.

In 1925 President Ebert died and Hindenburg became President. He was a hero of the First World War. He thought that Germany had been 'stabbed in the back' by the Weimar politicians who had signed the Treaty of Versailles.

??????????????

1 a What did Ludendorff think was 'a disgrace to Germany' (**A**)?
b How did Stresemann's aims (**B**) differ from those in **C**?
c List the changes in Germany's reparation payments between 1923 and 1929.

2 a What does **D** tell us about German industry in the 1920s?
b Draw a graph to show the information in **H**. What does your graph indicate about changes in the Reichstag?

3 Write an obituary for Stresemann from the point of view of either an opponent or a supporter.

4 What were the main strengths of the Weimar Republic in 1928?

H Some parties in the Reichstag 1920–28

Party	Number of seats			
	1920	**1924**	**1924**	**1928**
Communists	4	62	45	54
Social Democrats	103	100	131	153
Nazis	—	32	14	12

10 The Rise of Hitler and the Nazis

While Hitler was in jail after the Munich Putsch (see pages 18–19) he wrote a book about his life and ideas. It was called *Mein Kampf* (My Struggle). **A** shows the main arguments of the book:

A Key ideas in Hitler's 'Mein Kampf'

> **a** Struggle is the basis of history.
> **b** There is a struggle in the world between different races of people.
> **c** The main struggle that the German (or *Aryan*) race must fight is against the Jewish race.
> **d** The German race needs more land so that it can preserve itself and expand.
> **e** A strong nation must be united under a strong leader.

D Unable to afford a bed for the night, unemployed men sleep hunched over a rope

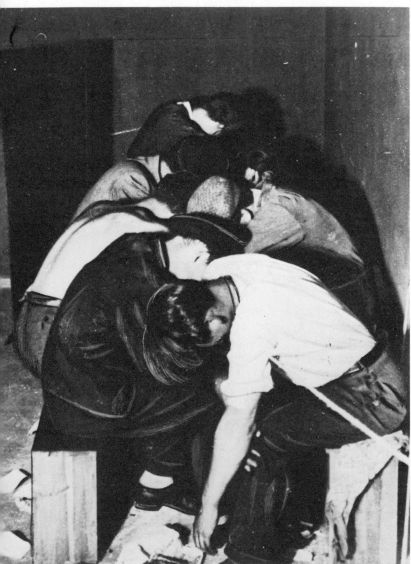

After the failure of the 1923 Putsch Hitler decided on a change in tactics. He wrote in a letter from prison in 1923:

'*When I resume active work, it will be necessary to pursue a new policy. Instead of working to achieve power by an armed coup, we will have to hold our noses and enter the Reichstag against the Catholic and Marxist members. If outvoting them takes longer than outshooting them, at least the result will be guaranteed by their own constitution. Any lawful process is slow. Sooner or later we will have a majority, and after that – Germany!*' **(B)**

When he was released from prison in December 1924 Hitler re-formed the Nazi Party. In 1928 the Nazis had only 12 representatives in the Reichstag. Hitler concentrated on building up the Party in the country. He looked to the middle classes and the farmers for support. He was helped by a fall in prices at this time, which hit farmers badly.

Hitler used rallies, speeches, attacks on his opponents and violence in the streets (led by the SA) to gain voters and supporters. In the rural area of Schleswig Holstein, support for the Nazis increased from 4 per cent of voters in 1928 to 27 per cent in the elections of 1930. Hitler got the support of other right-wing groups in the campaign against the Young Plan (see pages 20–21). People were beginning to accept him as a respectable political figure.

America was hit by the Depression at the end of the 1920s. American loans to Germany were withdrawn. This had serious effects on Germany. Unemployment rose sharply **(C)**. Many of the unemployed faced great hardship (see **D**).

The government of Chancellor Müller resigned in March 1930 and Brüning took over. It seemed impossible for anyone to get a majority in the Reichstag, or to organise a coalition. Article 48 of the Weimar constitution said that Germany could be ruled *by decree* (without the Reichstag) in times of emergency. Rule by decree became the normal form of government after 1930.

C Unemployment 1928–32

1928	1 862 000
1929	2 850 000
1930	3 217 000
1931	4 886 000
1932	6 042 000

1928	12
1930	107
1932 July	230 (largest party in the Reichstag)
1932 Nov	196

E Nazi seats in the Reichstag 1928–32

Date	Chancellor	Event
1932	Brüning	
10 April		Hindenburg re-elected President.
		SA and SS banned.
		Gröner, defence minister, resigned.
		Schleicher defence minister.
30 May		Schleicher persuaded Hindenburg to dismiss Brüning.
	Papen	
June		End of ban on SA and SS.
July		Prime Minister of Prussia removed.
		Hindenburg refused to make Hitler Chancellor.
		Elections to the Reichstag.
		Nazis strongest party.
		Papen government defeated in Reichstag.
November		New elections.
		Papen resigned.
	Schleicher	Schleicher failed to split the Nazis or win support.
1933		
January		Schleicher resigned.
22 January		Hindenburg agreed to make Hitler Chancellor.
30 January	Hitler	

F Timechart: April 1932 – January 1933

G A Nazi poster used in the 1932 election campaign

High unemployment put a strain on the government, as it had to pay out unemployment benefits. Many civil servants had their salaries cut. The unemployed got less dole. Those lucky enough to be in work could buy less with their wages. They had to pay more taxes. The Nazis and the Communists gained increasing numbers of seats in the elections of 1928–32 (**E**).

The SA had little time for slow 'legal tactics'. They wanted to seize power by force. Brüning hoped to stop this by banning the SA.

F shows the events of 1932–33. In 1932 Hindenburg had been in power for seven years. An election for the office of President was held. Hitler decided to stand in the election. But the Nazis were short of money. Hitler spoke to a meeting of German industrialists in Düsseldorf. Almost at once, money started coming in.

In the election on 13 March 1932 the Nazis won 33 per cent of the votes. Hindenburg won the election, but he did not have an absolute majority. So another election had to be held, on 10 April. This time, Hitler's

vote increased to 13 million. Hindenburg gained over 19 million votes, and was re-elected.

Rumours spread that the Nazis were planning a violent takeover. The government banned the SA and SS. On 30 May 1932 Defence Minister Schleicher persuaded Hindenburg to dismiss Brüning. Another Centre Party politician, Papen, became Chancellor. He tried to get the support of the Nazi Party by lifting the ban on the SA and taking over power from Social Democrats in Prussia. Hitler insisted that he would only support the government if he were made Chancellor.

The Nazis were by now the most powerful party in the Reichstag. In November, Papen was forced to resign. New elections were held. **G** is a Nazi election

MILLIONEN
stehen hinter mir

N 'Millions stand behind me'

poster. This time, the Nazis gained fewer seats, and some people thought the Party was finished. One commentator said:

Hitler is done for, the Nazi spell has been broken. **(H)**

In December, Schleicher became Chancellor. He tried to split up the Nazis but failed. In January 1933 Papen persuaded Hindenburg to appoint Hitler as Chancellor, to replace Schleicher. Three of Hitler's cabinet of 12 were Nazis.

How did people see Hitler at the time? This is what three German writers thought in 1932:

We (the Communists) lost the fight because we were not fishermen, as we thought, but bait dangling from a hook. **(J)**
Arthur Koestler

People laughed about him, perhaps not as much as in preceding years, but they certainly couldn't take the man seriously. **(K)**
Vicky Baum

we are, I believe, over the peak. The height of the madness seems to have been passed. **(L)**
Thomas Mann

M lists the factors that contributed to Hitler's rise to power.

M Reasons for Hitler's success

1 The Nazi Party was well organised.
2 People feared the Communists.
3 Hitler was a good speaker.
4 Few people liked the governments of the Weimar Republic.
5 Hitler's ideas were popular.
6 There was an agricultural depression.
7 There was mass unemployment.
8 Stresemann died in October 1929.
9 The Communists thought that the Social Democrats were a greater danger than the Nazis.
10 Industrialists supported Hitler (see **N**).

??????????????????

1 a What was 'Mein Kampf'?
b What were Hitler's aims for the German (Aryan) race (**A**)?
c How did Hitler's policy change after 1923 (**B**)?

2 a What does **E** tell us about support for the Nazis?
b What reasons can you suggest for the changes in **E**?

3 a What sort of people would poster **G** have appealed to? Why?
b Design a poster for the 1932 election campaign attacking the Nazi Party.

4 a Put the factors in **M** in your order of importance for helping Hitler to power. Give reasons for your order.
b What does the evidence suggest about people's view of Hitler at this time?

5 The Weimar Republic survived the crisis of 1923. Why did it fail to survive that of 1930–33?

11 A Berlin Suburb

How did the Lennhoffs and others feel about events in Weimar Germany from 1918–33? These are some of the people who lived in their Berlin suburb.

Mr Lennhoff (Friedrich Lennhoff's father) ran a factory which made ornamental ironwork and decorations for better off middle class Germans. In the factory worked a *young soldier* who had been wounded in the war. Gas had affected his lungs, his brothers had been killed, and when the war ended he felt utterly betrayed.

Near the Lennhoffs lived a *civil servant*. He was paid a regular wage, and supported his father and mother, both of whom received a small, regular pension. He was a Catholic and moderate in politics, and was opposed to the dictatorship of the Kaiser.

In the local school worked a *young teacher* who belonged to the Communist Party. She had been active in the Spartacist movement, but had not been arrested when it collapsed.

Next door to the Lennhoffs was an *industrialist* who owned an iron foundary. He had done well out of the war, and wanted stable conditions to get his factory back on to a prosperous footing.

Finally there was an unemployed *army officer*. He had fought bravely on the Russian front, and after the war had joined up with a number of ex-officers. They spent their time drinking and talking about the good old days under the Kaiser, before there was discontent and rioting; when there was plenty to eat for everyone. They were all members of the Freikorps.

How do you think each of these people would have reacted in June 1920, when the first general election under the new Weimar Republic was due to be held?

1 Would he/she have supported the Weimar Constitution?
2 Would he/she have backed the army in putting down street fighting?
3 Would he/she have supported a government freeze on all prices?

Discuss what each person would have felt and done. Then circle the answer in the chart below. For example, if you think the *young teacher* would have strongly supported the Weimar Constitution, circle 'a', and so on.

a = strongly support   c = not care
b = support   d = totally oppose

	Question 1				Question 2				Question 3			
Mr Lennhoff	a	b	c	d	a	b	c	d	a	b	c	d
Young soldier	a	b	c	d	a	b	c	d	a	b	c	d
Civil servant	a	b	c	d	a	b	c	d	a	b	c	d
Young teacher	a	b	c	d	a	b	c	d	a	b	c	d
Industrialist	a	b	c	d	a	b	c	d	a	b	c	d
Army officer	a	b	c	d	a	b	c	d	a	b	c	d

How might their views have changed by November 1923? Since 1921 the suburb had seen dramatic changes. Because of inflation the Lennhoff factory had taken to paying its workers daily. *Mr Lennhoff* is very aware of the rising tide of hatred directed against Jews. They are blamed for the inflation which made the pension of the *civil servant's* parents worthless. The *young soldier* has joined Adolf Hitler's Nazi party, and is proud to be one of its storm-troopers. Because the Lennhoffs are kind employers, he is not too happy about Hitler's attacks on the Jews.

The *young teacher* is in despair, and can afford only a few cheap vegetables to feed herself on. The *industrialist* was doing very well out of inflation, with his factories and the ownership of a farm. However, the occupation of the Ruhr has meant that he has lost his most important ironworks. It is now in French hands. The *army officer* took part in the Kapp putsch. His pension is now worthless, and he is thinking of joining the Nazi party.

How do you think each person might answer these questions (draw up a chart and ring your answers in the same way as for questions 1–3):

4 Would he/she blame the Jews and the Versailles settlement for the troubles of 1923 – the great inflation and the occupation of the Ruhr?

5 Would he/she back a party that would rebuild Germany's armed forces and try to regain control of the Rhineland?

6 Would he/she support the Nazi revolt in Munich?

Now look back at pages 20–21 and 22–23. Imagine the reaction of these figures to the events from 1923–33. (Fill out a third chart and ring your answers.)

7 Would he/she support the foreign policy of Stresemann?
8 Would he/she support the Nazis in 1928?
9 Would he/she support the Nazis in 1930?
10 Would he/she be in favour of Hitler becoming Chancellor?

12 Hitler and Nazi Germany

What do you know about Hitler? Write down or tell your neighbour what first comes to mind when you think about Hitler. West German schoolchildren were asked to do this in 1977. **A** shows some of their answers. How many of them do you think were right?

❝Hitler was strong.

He drank lots of whisky and sang songs.

Adolf Hitler was an Italian.

Adolf Hitler was highly intelligent, he built up industry and put new heart into the people after a lost war.

I think he was born in 1819.

Hitler came to power through a putsch.❞ **(A)**

Table **B** shows the main events in Hitler's life.

The evidence on these pages tells us more about Hitler. Look at each piece of evidence carefully, and ask yourself the following questions:

Is it *primary* (first-hand) or *secondary* (second-hand) evidence?

Is it biased (one-sided) in any way? How?

What does it tell us about Hitler?

How does this fit in with what we already know/the other evidence?

C is a German woodcut, called 'The Third Reich', made in 1934. **D–J** are some of the things that have been written or said about Hitler.

❝I shall go down in history as the greatest German.❞ **(D)**

(Hitler, speaking on 15 March 1939)

Stern

C 'The Third Reich', 1934

B Adolf Hitler 1889–1945

1889	Born at Braunau-am-Inn, Austria. Educated at Linz, Austria.
1909–13	Lived in Vienna.
1914	Moved to Germany, joined the Bavarian army. Fought in World War I and won the Iron Cross.
1919	Joined Munich workers' group which became the National Socialist Workers' Party (NSDAP).
1923	Unsuccessful Munich putsch. Hitler jailed. Wrote *Mein Kampf* in jail.
1933	*30 January* Hitler made head of German government.
1934	*August* Hitler made Führer (leader of German Reich).
1939	*September* Outbreak of World War II.
1944	*July* Assassination attempt on Hitler.
1945	Married his mistress, Eva Braun. *30 April* Shot himself.

❝I often make up my mind to say something to him, but then when I come face to face with him my heart sinks into my boots.❞ **(E)** (Schacht, Head of German Reichsbank, quoting Göring)

❝. . . in the years 1938–41, at the height of his success, he had succeeded in persuading a great part of the German nation that in him they had found a ruler of more than human qualities, a man of genius raised up by Providence to lead them into the Promised Land.❞ **(F)** (Alan Bullock, a British historian)

❝Adolf Hitler enters a hall. He sniffs the air. For a minute he gropes, feels his way, senses the atmosphere. Suddenly he bursts forth. His words go like an arrow to their target, he touches each private wound on the raw, liberating the mass unconscious, expressing the innermost aspirations, telling it what it most wants to hear.❞ **(G)** (Otto Strasser, a Nazi leader)

"Hitler stamped his feet, and banged his fist on tables and walls. He foamed at the mouth, panting and stammering in uncontrolled fury." **(H)** (Hermann Rauschning, *Hitler Speaks*, 1939)

"(He) knew what he was speaking about and, as the long interviews proceeded, showed himself completely master of his subject." **(J)** (The Earl of Avon, 1962)

K and **L** are photographs of Hitler.

We know that Nazi policies resulted in a world war, and the deliberate killing of millions of people. But historians have different ideas about how this could happen in a 'civilised' country.

- Some say that Hitler had total control over Germany. It was a *totalitarian* state.
- Some see the Nazi Party as just one of several similar movements in Europe at the time (eg in Spain and Italy). These movements are known as *fascism*. (Mussolini's followers in Italy called themselves fascists.)

- Some believe that Hitler did not have total control over Germany. Nazi policies were the result of different groups struggling for power.

Even today, historians continue to discuss these issues. **M** comes from a newspaper report on a conference held in 1984:

"The holocaust's hardest question . . .

In an atmosphere of eerie intensity, an extraordinary gathering of 200 eminent historians and experts on Nazi Germany convened in the old city of Stuttgart last week. They met to discuss with grimly determined dispassion their most passionately held and widely differing beliefs on the greatest trauma of the 20th century: the holocaust and how the horror came about.

There is a deep split between two schools of thought. The "intentionalists" believe that the wholesale murder of European Jewry and other minorities sprang from a master plan drawn up by Hitler even before he came to power. Their opponents, the "functionalists", hold that it developed gradually. They say it was, in part at least, dictated — with Hitler's knowledge and approval, of course — by political and logistic expedients beyond the Führer's immediate control." **(M)**

(The Sunday Times, 6 May 1984)

K Hitler posing with German children in 1936

L Hitler ceremonially beginning work on Germany's first Autobahn

13 The 'Nazi Revolution'

The Reichstag Fire

27 February 1933. Passers-by saw flames coming from the *Reichstag* (parliament building) in Berlin. The Vice-Chancellor, von Papen, was dining with President Hindenburg. Papen later wrote:

> *Suddenly we noticed a red glow through the windows and heard sounds of shouting in the street. One of the servants came hurrying up to me and whispered: "The Reichstag is on fire!"* (A)

Someone who was standing closer to the fire remembered:

> *I was standing about 40 or 50 metres away from the flames which blazed in the night sky. While I was standing around with my former colleagues, Göring told the press spokesman to report "The Communists have set fire to the Reichstag".* (B)

C The Reichstag building in flames

C shows what people saw that evening.

Egon Larsen listened to the radio to find out more:

> *There was a news bulletin . . . just issued by the official press service. One man had been arrested in the building shortly after nine o'clock by a police constable; firelighters and petrol-soaked rags were found on him. He was identified as a 24-year-old Dutchman, a bricklayer by the name of Marinus van der Lubbe. He had, said the radio, admitted that he was a Communist . . .* (D)

People are not sure how the fire started, but van der Lubbe was blamed and executed. Hitler used the fire as an excuse to arrest 4000 Communists. He also persuaded President Hindenburg to sign the 'Emergency Decree for the Protection of the People and State'. This meant that the police could arrest people suspected of a crime, and imprison them without trial. The government banned left-wing newspapers.

Hitler was getting ready for the elections on 5 March 1933. Cartoon E shows what the British newspaper, the *Daily Express* thought about the elections. F shows the election results.

The government held a ceremony to celebrate the opening of the new parliament on 21 March 1933, at Potsdam, outside Berlin. Hitler wanted his takeover of power to appear to be legal. He also wanted to pass a law which would allow *(enable)* him to rule without the Reichstag. He needed to get two thirds of the members of parliament to agree to this in order to get it passed. He arrested more Communists and Social Democrats. The Centre Party thought it safest to support the Nazis.

With all Communist members of parliament under arrest, the only votes against the 'Enabling Law' were those of 94 Social Democrats. The Act was passed on 24 March 1933. It gave the government powers to make laws without the agreement of parliament.

Hitler then went on to ban the Social Democrats on 22 June. On 5 July the Centre Party broke up. Hitler passed another law on 14 July 1933, which said:

> *The National Socialist German Workers' Party is the only political party in Germany.* (G)

Germany was now a 'one-party state'.

Hitler next tried to get control over other areas of life in Germany (H). This was called co-ordination *(Gleichschaltung)*.

E Cartoon from the British *Daily Express*, 4 March 1933

Party	Number of seats
Communists	81
Social Democrats	120
Centre	74
Nazis	288
Others	84

F Results of the election of 5 March 1933

Civil Service Law: Jews could be sacked from civil service.
Legal system: Judges had to join a Nazi organisation. A 'People's Court' was set up.
Trade Unions: Were closed down in May 1933.
German states: Their parliaments were replaced by Reich governors.

H Hitler's plans to 'co-ordinate' German life

Night of the Long Knives

Some people wanted the 'Nazi revolution' to go further. Ernst Röhm, the leader of the SA, wrote in June 1933:

❝*The SA and SS will not tolerate the German revolution going to sleep . . . we will continue our struggle.*❞ (J)

Others were afraid that things were going too far:

❝*everyone is arresting everyone else . . . these present circumstances must inevitably lead to chaos.*❞ (K) (a local SS leader)

Hitler wanted to stop the SA getting too powerful. There was talk of an SA plot to seize power. Hitler needed the support of the army, and they objected to the SA. On 29 June 1934 Hitler called a meeting of SA leaders at Wiessee in Bavaria for the next day. Hitler's chauffeur wrote about the events of 30 June:

❝*Hitler sits down beside me and gives the order:*
"To Wiessee, as fast as possible!"
It must have been about 4.30 am, the sky has cleared up, it is nearly bright daylight . . .
Just before Wiessee, Hitler suddenly breaks his silence:
"Kempka," he says, "drive carefully when we come to the Hotel Hanselbauer. You must drive up without making any noise. If you see an SA guard in front of the hotel, don't wait for them to report to me; drive on and stop at the hotel entrance." Then, after a moment of deathly silence:
"Röhm wants to carry out a coup."
An icy shiver ran down my back. I could have believed anything, but not a coup by Röhm!❞ (L)

Röhm was arrested and a revolver left in his cell. He refused to use it, so the SS (see page 30) shot him. In Berlin, Schleicher and his wife were shot at their home. Papen's office was wrecked. The SS executed many SA leaders, as well as the private enemies of Hitler. The body of Kahr, who had let Hitler down at the time of the Munich Putsch in 1923, was found in a swamp. Hitler called the night of 29/30 June the *Night of the Long Knives*. On that night and during the next few days up to 400 people were killed. Hitler now had tighter control over the Nazi party.

On 2 August 1934 President Hindenburg died. Hitler took over the powers of the President and made himself Führer and Reich Chancellor. Soldiers and officials had to swear an oath to be loyal to him.

??????????????

1 a Is there anything suspicious about Göring's statement in **B**?
b How was the Reichstag fire useful to Hitler?
c Use evidence **A–D** to prepare an 'official' radio broadcast about the fire.

2 According to **E**, how did the Nazis get people to vote for them? Do you think this gives a true picture of Nazi elections?

3 a Why did Hitler attack the SA?
b Why did he tell the driver to be quiet (**L**)?
c How far can we trust **L**?

4 What methods did Hitler use to strengthen his position between 30 January 1933 and 2 August 1934? What problems still faced him at the end of this period?

29

14 Terror!

1925	Hitler set up SS as a bodyguard.
1929	Heinrich Himmler became leader of SS.
1933	SS carried out arrests after Reichstag Fire.
	SS set up concentration camps.
1934	SS carried out executions on the 'Night of the Long Knives'.
1939	SS special squads ('Einsatzgruppen') started mass killings in the lands occupied by Germany.

A Actions by the SS 1925–39

Hitler used terror to keep his opponents quiet. As well as sparking off violence on the streets (see pages 22–24), he carried out a highly organised terror campaign. The SS (Schutzstaffel/stormtroop) became the main force for carrying out the terror (see **A**).

After the Reichstag Fire the SS set up *concentration camps* where they could keep prisoners. The most important of these camps was Dachau, near Munich.

B comes from the regulations at Dachau concentration camp:

❝*The following are punishable with two weeks solitary confinement:*
1 Anyone exchanging . . . the quarters to which he is assigned.
2 Anyone enclosing or hiding forbidden articles, or articles produced in the camp, in outgoing laundry bundles, or sewing them into pieces of laundry, etc.
3 Anyone entering or leaving barracks, shelters, or other buildings by other than authorised entrances, or creeping through windows or other openings.
4 Anyone smoking in shelters, toilets and places which are fire hazards, or keeping or depositing inflammable objects in such places . . .

The following offenders will be hanged. Anyone who does the following in the camp, at work, in the sleeping quarters, in the kitchens and workshops, toilets and places of rest: discusses politics, carries on controversial talks and meetings, forms cliques; loiters around with others; who for the purpose of

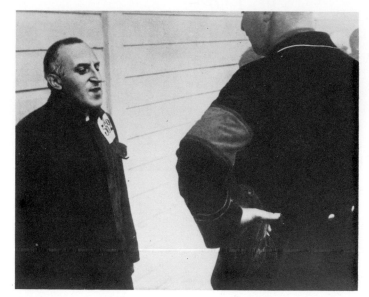

D Carl Von Ossietzky in Esterwegen concentration camp

supplying the propaganda of the opposition with atrocity stories, collects true or false information about the concentration camp . . . All punishments will be recorded on files ❞ (**B**)

Prisoners had to wear a triangular piece of coloured cloth on their uniforms. The colours showed what sort of prisoner they were (**C**).

The Nazis arrested anyone who opposed them. They jailed the Nobel peace prize winner Carl Von Ossietzky (**D**). A representative of the Red Cross wrote report **E** after visiting Ossietzky in a concentration camp.

❝*He hardly seemed to be alive. He was shaking and deadly pale. He did not seem to feel anything. One eye was swollen, his teeth had been knocked out, his leg was broken . . .* ❞ (**E**)

F shows the number of prisoners estimated to be in concentration camps between 1933 and 1939. The size of the camps grew enormously after 1939.

C The Nazi state had no place for these groups – they were sent to concentration camps

Political Prisoners	red
Jehovah's Witnesses	purple
Anti-Socials	black
Criminals	green
Homosexuals	pink
Emigrants	blue
Jews	yellow star

F Estimated number of prisoners in concentration camps

Year	No. of prisoners	Deaths
1933	50 000	6250
1934	56 250	7300
1935	65 850	7900
1936	71 150	8500
1937	76 850	9200
1938	83 050	33 200
1939	132 900	66 450

15 Propaganda

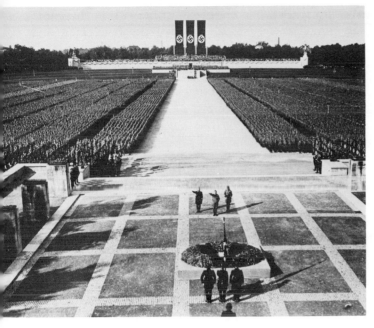

B Hitler at a mass rally in Nuremberg, 1934

As well as using terror as a weapon against his enemies, Hitler used *propaganda* to influence people's thoughts. Albert Speer, Nazi Armaments Minister in the Second World War, pointed out the power of the Nazi propaganda:

❝*Through technical devices like the radio and the loudspeaker, 80 million people were deprived of independent thought. It was thereby possible to subject them to the will of one man . . .*❞ (A)

The radio was probably Hitler's most important tool. The Nazi government put cheap radios on the market. They set up radios in factories and meeting places. In 1933 4.5 million households had a radio. By 1945 16 million had one.

Another form of propaganda was the mass rally (B). The American journalist William Shirer went to a rally in 1934:

❝*"We are strong and will get stronger," Hitler shouted at them through the microphone, his words echoing across the hushed field from the loudspeakers. And there in the floodlit night, jammed together like sardines, in one mass formation, the little men of Germany who have made Nazism possible achieved the highest state of being the German man knows . . . they were merged completely in the Germanic herd.*❞ (C)

In March 1933 Hitler set up a 'Ministry for People's Enlightenment and Propaganda' led by Dr Joseph Goebbels. Goebbels took over Nazi propaganda. He said:

❝*It is the task of State propaganda so to simplify complicated ways of thinking that even the smallest man in the street may understand.*❞ (D)

In 1940 he commented:

❝*the fundamental principle of all propaganda (is) the repetition of effective arguments . . .*❞ (E)

and later,

❝*. . . lies must be used only as a defensive measure and not for making a false show of success.*❞ (F)

The Propaganda Ministry held press conferences each day to 'guide' the press. **G** and **H** are two of the 'guidelines' they issued:

❝*Photos showing members of the Reich government at dining tables in front of rows of bottles must not be published in future . . .*❞ (G)   (6 April 1935)

❝*The Minister criticises most sharply the publication by "Die Woche" of a picture of the record from which the radio transmits the fanfare preceding the special announcements.*❞ (H)

(9 June 1940)

??????????????????

1 a Use the evidence on page 30 to write brief notes on life in a Nazi concentration camp. You should mention: rules; punishments; physical conditions; other prisoners; deaths.
b Which piece of evidence in this section is most useful to an historian investigating the concentration camps? Why?

2 a List the propaganda techniques that might be used at a mass rally (**B**, **C**) e.g. floodlights, banners . . .)
b What three points did Goebbels make about the use of propaganda in **D**, **E** and **F**?
c Why was the Propaganda Ministry worried about the pictures mentioned in **G** and **H**?

3 Imagine you are an adviser to Hitler in the 1930s. Which means of controlling people (concentration camps; terror; radio; education; rallies . . .) would you most recommend him to use, and why?

16 The Persecution of the Jews

Much of the Nazi terror and propaganda (see pages 30–31) was directed against Jewish people. In *Mein Kampf* (see pages 22–24) Hitler blamed the Jews for the evil in the world, and said that the German race would have to struggle against the Jewish race. He blamed the defeat of Germany in the First World War on the Jews:

If, at the beginning and during the war, someone had only subjected about 12 or 15 000 of these Hebrew enemies of the people to poison gas . . . then the sacrifice of millions at the front would not have been in vain. **(A)**

By 1945 the Nazis had killed 70 per cent of European Jews (about six million people).

Hitler attacked the Jews in the 1933 Nazi party election manifesto and in his speeches. When he came to power life became more difficult for Jews. Hannele Zürndorfer, a child at the time, remembers:

The papers all carried cartoons lampooning (making fun of) the Jews with enormous, grotesque noses, furtive or greedy faces and big, slobbering lips . . . At first I only sensed that I was less welcome in the street games; then some of the other children became actively hostile, teasing and baiting me and pushing me about when I was on roller-skates, so that I no longer liked going out to play. **(B)**

At first, Hitler had to keep the support of as many people as possible, especially abroad. He could not afford to get rid of Jews from industry. Some Nazi groups, like the SA, wanted to attack the Jews straight away. In 1933 the government told people not to shop at Jewish shops. Many people ignored this 'boycott'. Jews were told that they could not do government jobs. They were not allowed in some public places.

Just before a huge Nazi Party rally in Nuremberg in 1935 Hitler and his advisers worked out some laws against Jews. They scribbled these down on menu cards, as there was not enough paper at hand. C shows extracts from the *Nuremberg Laws* of 15 September 1935:

1 Marriages between Jews and citizens of German or kindred blood are forbidden . . .
2 Sexual relations outside marriage between Jews and nationals of German and kindred blood are forbidden.
3 Jews will not be permitted to employ female citizens of German or kindred blood as domestic servants. **(C)**

The government passed other laws to define who was Jewish, and to restrict what Jews could do. In 1936 the Olympic Games were held in Berlin. Hitler tried to cover up the Nazi anti-Jewish policy while the games were on. But afterwards attacks on Jews increased. Hannele Zürndorfer was getting frightened:

I wanted to cut out the grey, fearsome streets with jackbooted Brownshirts (the SA) who stamped about like robots, marching, shouting, saluting, red-faced with wild and bloodshot eyes. At least, that is how they appeared to me. Danger was outside. At home we were safe – I thought. **(D)**

On 7 November 1938 a Polish Jew shot an official in the German Embassy in Paris. Goebbels encouraged Nazis to take their revenge. Hannele's worst fears became true on 9–10 November 1938:

It must have been three or four o'clock in the morning, when suddenly I was ripped out of my sleep by the sound of smashing crockery and glass . . . Seconds later there burst into this room a horde of violent monsters . . . They were wielding axes, sledgehammers, stones and knives. They rushed about the room smashing, throwing, trampling. **(E)**

That night became known as the *Kristallnacht* (Crystal Night or Night of the Broken Glass). All over Germany, Nazis attacked property belonging to Jews (**F**) and synagogues (**G**). A Nazi report said that 91 Jews were killed and 20 000 arrested. The Nazi press said that this was a:

F Shops belonging to Jews were looted

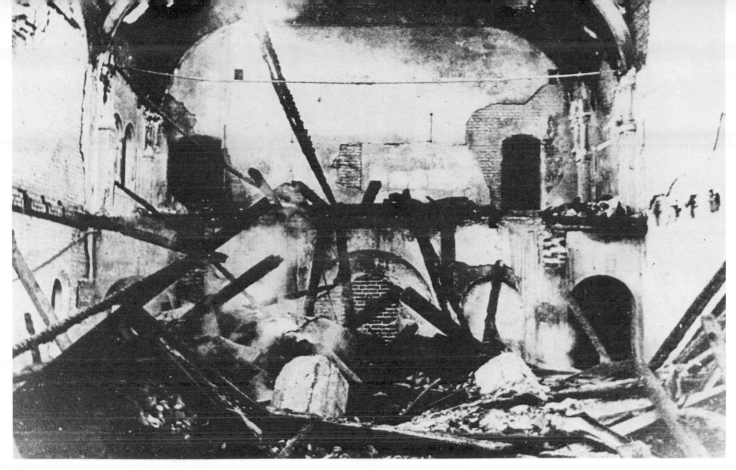

G A burnt-out synagogue in Munich

❝*spontaneous wave of righteous indignation throughout Germany, as a result of the cowardly Jewish murder of Third Secretary von Rath in the German Embassy at Paris.*❞ **(H)**

According to an American observer, most German people did not know what was happening. The damage was caused:

❝*by SS men and Stormtroopers not in uniform, each group having been provided with hammers, axes, crowbars and incendiary bombs.*❞ **(J)**

Some Nazi leaders were worried by the effects of the action. Göring called a meeting of Nazi leaders on 12 November. **K** is taken from an account of this meeting:

❝Göring: *"If today a Jewish shop is destroyed and goods are thrown into the street, the insurance company will pay for the damage, which does not even touch the Jew . . ."*
Goebbels: *"My advice is that the Jew should be eliminated from any position in public life . . . It is still possible today for a Jew to share a compartment in a sleeping car with a German . . . we need a decree stating that separate compartments shall be available to Jews . . ."*
Göring: *"I'd give the Jews one coach or one compartment. And should . . . the train be overcrowded, believe me, we won't need a law. We'll kick him out and he'll have to sit all alone in the lavatory all the way."*❞ **(K)**

The government passed a law to make Jews pay for the damage done in the Kristallnacht. Signs prohibiting Jews appeared in even more places. Jews lost their property. Some Jews, like Hannele Zürndorfer, left Germany, others stayed on. After 1939 Hitler's persecution of the Jews took a new turn (see pages 44–45).

??????????????

1 Make a timechart showing Nazi anti-Jewish policy, 1933–9. Alongside each event, write what you think Hannele Zürndorfer would have felt about it.

2 What factors stopped Hitler from launching a full-scale attack on the Jews until 1939?

3 a Why were the buildings in **F** and **G** attacked?
b Why did Göring and Goebbels want to take a tough line against the Jews (**K**)?
c Use the evidence in **E–J** to write a short account of the Kristallnacht. Mention: what happened; who was responsible; reasons for and effects of the violence.

4 Make up a conversation between Hannele and her family about whether they should leave Germany or stay. What factors would influence their decision?

17 The Economy

A Celebrations to mark the opening of a new Autobahn

Hitler had promised his supporters work and bread. In 1933 he was faced with six million unemployed. To stay in power he needed to find them jobs. Four policies he could follow were to:

- attack department stores and make them lower prices.
- get rid of Jewish industrialists and give their firms to Germans.
- attack big business, and make it do what the government wanted.
- continue the work creation schemes started by previous governments.

At first, Hitler followed the last plan. He decided to build up the *Autobahn* (motorway) network in Germany. He planned 7000 kilometres of motorway. By 1938, 3000 kilometres had been built. **A** shows the opening of a new Autobahn. In 1935 Hitler brought back compulsory service in the army *(conscription)*, and introduced a Labour Service. This meant that all men between 18 and 26 had to serve six months in public work camps (**B**). Women had to do domestic or farm work. **C** shows what happened to unemployment levels between 1933 and 1939.

B Young men at a public work camp

1933	6 million
1934	3.7 million
1936	2.5 million
1937	1.8 million
1938	1 million
1939	300 000

C Unemployment 1933–39

1928	100
1933	66
1934	83
1935	96
1937	117
1938	125
1939	132

E Industrial production in Germany 1928–39

F How Hitler's economic policy worked

On gaining power, Hitler had said:

❛*Everything must be for the armed forces. Germany's position in the world depends decisively upon the position of the German armed forces. The position of the German economy in the world is also dependent on that.*❜ (**D**)

To build up the army, Hitler needed to strengthen German industry (**E**). In its turn, strengthening the army helped the German economy (**F**).

In August 1936 Hitler wrote:

❛*If we are not able in the shortest possible time to make the German Wehrmacht* (army) *in training, in the disposition of its formations, and, above all, in its psychological readiness, the first army in the world, then Germany will be lost! To the achievement of this goal, all other considerations must be unconditionally subordinated. The German Army must be operational in four years. The German economy must be capable of supporting war in four years.*❜ (**G**)

How should Hitler carry out his 'Four Year Plan'? **H** shows some of the available options. **J** shows the factors Hitler had to consider before making his decision.

For Hitler the choice was simple. He said in 1943 (talking about his policies in the 1930s):

❛*Our armaments have swallowed fantastic sums . . . There are only two ways: either these debts will be put on the shoulders of the people in the Reich in the shape of taxes, or they will be paid for by the possible profits from the occupied eastern territories.*❜ (**K**)

Hitler chose the second way. By 1939 his army was ready to attack in the East.

1 Raise taxes.
2 Cut imports from abroad.
3 Reduce wages and make working hours longer.
4 Take labour and raw materials from other countries.

H Options

a A successful war might make Hitler more popular.
b Important raw materials can be found in Czechoslovakia.
c If imports are cut there will be fewer goods in the shops.
d Other countries may object if Hitler moves into Czechoslovakia.
e There is a shortage of skilled workers.
f Industrial workers are already unhappy about working conditions. They want greater rewards for their work.
g Higher taxes will be unpopular.

J Considerations

???????????????

1 a What was the main problem facing Hitler in 1933?
b What plan did he decide to follow? Why?
c List the ways by which Hitler tried to tackle unemployment.
d How successful was he (**C**)?

2 Describe in detail what you can see in **A** and **B**. What can photographs like this tell us about Hitler and Nazi Germany?

3 a What was the main aim of Hitler's economic policy (see **D** and **F**)?
b How could building motorways and strengthening industry help rearmament?
c Why did Hitler introduce the Four Year Plan in 1936 (**G**)?

4 Look at **H** and **J**. Match up the considerations with the options they affect (e.g. 1 and (g)). Which options would you have advised Hitler to follow in 1936? Why? Which plan did Hitler eventually adopt? Why do you think he chose it? What were the advantages and disadvantages of this policy?

18 People

B Nazi youth movements stressed the importance of health and fitness. Girls took part in gymnastics displays

A The Hitler Youth on parade

What was life like in Nazi Germany? The evidence in this section suggests what life would have been like for some different types of people in Nazi Germany before 1939.

A young person would probably join a Nazi youth organisation. *14–18-year-old* boys joined the *Hitler Youth* (**A**) and girls the *League of German Girls* (**B**). Camping was very important for the Hitler Youth. C is from a plan for a camp.

❛*Friday, 10 July Password: Adolf Hitler. Motto for the day: Hitler is Germany and Germany is Hitler. Words: We owe to our leader Adolf Hitler the fact that we can open our camp today. Song: Onward, onward . . . Community hour: is omitted since the group is still very tired.*❜ (**C**)

At school, subjects like sport, history and biology were important. In December 1934 the Minister of the Interior announced:

❛*Teachers and pupils are to give one another the German salute* (the Hitler salute) *within and outside the school.*❜ (**D**)

Weeks	Subject	The Jews	Reading
1–4	Pre-War Germany.	The Jew at large!	Hauptmann's 'The Weavers'.
17–20	The Stab in the Back. Collapse.	The November Insurrection.	
25–28	Adolf Hitler. National Socialism.	Judah's foe!	Mein Kampf.

E A Nazi view of German history

Hitler set up some new schools to train young people to serve Nazi Germany. These were known as Adolf Hitler Schools, Ordensburgen and Party High Schools.

The teacher had to change his teaching to suit the Nazi government. E is taken from a Nazi history syllabus.

Some teachers were faced with difficult choices. A Berlin pupil said about her teacher:

He had a bad conscience. He tried to do two things. On the one hand he went out of his way to teach history from the Nazi point of view – there were three girls who belonged to the League of German Girls in the class who could have grassed (informed) on him . . . On the other hand he worked for the three Jews to be allowed to take the school leaving exam, he gave them good marks. That is the only thing he dared do. (F)

A woman These are some comments by Nazi leaders:

"The woman belongs to the smaller word . . . her husband, her family, her children and her home."

". . . Woman has her battlefield too; with each child that she brings into the world for the nation she is fighting her fight on behalf of the nation." (Hitler)

"Woman has the task of being beautiful and bringing children into the world . . ." (Goebbels) (G)

A factory worker German workers were encouraged to join the German Labour Front. 'Strength through Joy' (*Kraft durch Freude*) provided leisure activities such as films and excursions. Many workers had voted for the Social Democrats or Communists rather than the Nazis, but were pleased to see that there were more jobs and better pay after 1933.

In 1936 there was a shortage of butter, fats, eggs and meat. Prices went up. Wages stayed the same. Nazi reports spoke of "a growing ill-feeling against government and party". Social Democrats reported:

feverish unrest in all sections of the population . . . one can ask whom one wants to, all sections of the population are against the system. One can only wonder that this government can still exist. (H)

The farmer had voted for the Nazis on 5 March 1933. He hoped that they would help him. He was unhappy with the Farm Law in September 1933, because it made it difficult to do what you wanted with your land. He found it difficult to get farm workers after 1936. He feared Communism.

The army officer hated the Treaty of Versailles. He did not like the power of the SA in 1933. He hoped that Hitler would make the German army strong again.

The civil servant was willing to support anything that was legal. J is a popular joke about civil servants in Nazi Germany:

A stranger passing through a village notices a weather vane being taken down from a church steeple. He asks the workmen "Are you going to put a new one up?" "Oh, no, we're replacing it with a civil servant. A civil servant knows better than any weather vane which way the wind is blowing and which way he has got to turn." (J)

The Catholic hoped that the rights of Catholics would be upheld. He hoped that the *Concordat* (agreement) between the Catholic Church and the Nazi Party, signed in July 1933, would protect Catholics. He was upset by the removal of the *crucifix* (cross) from school-rooms in 1936.

?????????????????

1 a Draw up a table like the one below, to show how the people in this section might have reacted to the following: **1** Hitler becomes Chancellor; **2** Reichstag Fire; **3** Night of the Long Knives; **4** concentration camps; **5** Nuremberg Laws; **6** Kristallnacht; **7** motorways; **8** Hitler's Four Year Plan; **9** conscription; **10** Anschluss. Rate their reactions on a scale of a–e:
a – strongly like; b – like; c – don't care; d – dislike; e – strongly dislike.

Person	Events									
	1	2	3	4	5	6	7	8	9	10
Young person Teacher Woman										

b Make up interviews with three of the people, in which they explain the reasons for their reactions.

2 Use evidence **A–F** to describe what it would have been like to grow up in Nazi Germany.

3 List the different kinds of evidence in this section. How useful would each of them be to the historian?

19 Steps to War

Hitler wrote about the aims of his foreign policy in *Mein Kampf*:

‹*What a use could be made of the Treaty of Versailles! . . . How each one of the points of that Treaty could be branded in the minds and hearts of the German people until 60 million men and women find their souls aflame with a feeling of rage and shame; and a torrent of fire bursts forth as from a furnace, and a will of steel is forged from it, with the common cry: We will have arms again!*› (A)

Hitler wanted to abolish the Treaty. He even wrote:

‹*To demand that the 1914 frontiers of Germany should be restored is a political absurdity.*› (B)

These frontiers did not include all 'members of the German nation' since Germans also lived in Austria and Czechoslovakia. In 1933, on gaining power, the Nazi party programme demanded *Lebensraum* (living space). By this, it meant:

‹*land and territory for the nourishment of our people and for settling of surplus population.*› (C)

In October 1933 Hitler announced that Germany was not being treated as an equal by other countries. He withdrew Germany from the League of Nations. He asked the Germans to support him. On 12 November he held a vote on the matter (*a plebiscite*). 92 per cent of Germans agreed with his policy.

D German expansion by March 1939

```
areas taken over
by Germany by
March 1939
```

NORTH SEA
BALTIC SEA
POLISH CORRIDOR
EAST PRUSSIA
NETHERLANDS
POLAND
BELGIUM
RHINELAND & SAAR
GERMANY
LUX.
SUDETENLAND
CZECHOSLOVAKIA
FRANCE
AUSTRIA
HUNGARY
SWITZERLAND

H Cheering crowds welcomed Hitler at Graz, Austria

In July 1934 Austrian Nazis shot the Austrian leader, Dollfuss. Hitler hoped for Nazism to spread to Austria, but the plot failed. In January 1935 a plebiscite over the future of the Saar was held. 90 per cent of voters in the Saar wanted it to be joined to Germany (see map **D**).

In 1935 Hitler broke the Treaty of Versailles when he set up a German airforce (which the Treaty had prohibited), and announced *conscription* (compulsory military service). Other countries were slow to see the danger of Germany. For example, on 18 June 1935, Britain signed a naval agreement with Germany. Hitler broke the Versailles Treaty again when on 7 March 1936 German soldiers marched into the Rhineland (see map **D**). Hitler commented on this later:

‹*The 48 hours after the march into the Rhineland were the most nerve-racking in my life. If the French had then marched into the Rhineland we would have had to withdraw with our tails between our legs, for the military resources at our disposal would have been wholly inadequate for even a moderate resistance.*› (E)

Other countries protested but did not declare war on Germany. A Social Democrat described how the German people felt:

‹*everybody thought that there was some justification in Hitler's demands. All Germans hated Versailles. Hitler tore up this hateful treaty and forced France to its knees . . . people said 'he's got the courage to take risks'.*› (F)

Another plebiscite on 29 March 1936 won Hitler 98.8 per cent support. When the Spanish Civil War broke out in 1936 Hitler tried out his new airforce. He also looked for allies abroad and made alliances with Italy (*Rome–Berlin Axis*) and Japan (*Anti-Comintern Pact*).

On 5 November 1937 Hitler declared:

❝our first objective, in the event of our being embroiled in war, must be to overthrow Czechoslovakia and Austria . . . the annexation of Czechoslovakia and Austria would mean an acquisition of foodstuffs for five–six million people.❞ (G)

Hitler threatened to attack Austria. He forced the Austrian Chancellor, Schuschnigg, to take Nazis into his government. On 11 March 1938 German troops marched into Austria (H).

A plebiscite was held over the unification *(Anschluss)* of Austria and Germany. 99 per cent of people in Austria and Germany voted for the Anschluss. England and France protested, but took no action. Hitler had won without a fight. Now he demanded that Germans living in the Sudetenland (see D) should be brought into the German Reich. The Czech government refused to agree to this. England, France, Italy and Germany met on 29 September 1938 at Munich to discuss the Czech crisis. They accepted Hitler's demands. On 1 October 1938 German troops marched into the Sudetenland.

Not content with this, Hitler went on to occupy the rest of Bohemia and Moravia in March 1939.

Hitler now looked towards Poland. Danzig was a German-speaking city which the Treaty of Versailles had put under the control of the League of Nations. East Prussia was cut off from Germany by the 'Polish Corridor'. On 22 May 1939 Hitler signed an alliance with Italy. On 23 May he told his senior commanders:

❝Further successes cannot be achieved without bloodshed. Poland will always be on the side of our enemies . . . Danzig is not the objective. It is a matter of expanding our living space in the east . . . the decision remains to attack Poland at the first suitable opportunity.❞ (J)

On 23 August 1939 Hitler surprised many people by signing a treaty with the USSR (K) in which they agreed not to attack each other. They also agreed to divide Poland between them. On 1 September 1939 German troops invaded Poland.

Chart L shows Hitler's foreign policy.

L Hitler's foreign policy

1933	Germany leaves League of Nations.
1934	Non-aggression pact with Poland.
1935	*January* Saar plebiscite.
	March Conscription re-introduced.
	June Naval agreement with Britain.
1936	*March* Occupation of Rhineland.
	July Agreement with Austria.
	August Olympic Games in Berlin.
	Berlin–Rome Axis (with Italy).
	November Anti-Comintern Pact (with Japan).
1937	*November* Living space to be won by force.
1938	Supreme Command of armed forces set up
	Ribbentrop becomes Foreign Minister.
	March Germans into Austria.
	September Munich Conference.
	October German troops into Sudetenland.
1939	*March* German troops into Bohemia and Moravia Memel joined to Germany.
	May 'Pact of Steel' with Italy.
	August Nazi–Soviet Pact.
	September Germany invades Poland.

K A British cartoon on the Nazi–Soviet Pact, 1939

THE SCUM OF THE EARTH. I BELIEVE?

THE BLOODY ASSASSIN OF THE WORKERS I PRESUME?

??????????????????

1 a According to Hitler in **A**, what did the German people think about the Versailles Treaty? How accurate was he?

b Why did Hitler think that the Versailles Treaty was wrong (**A** and **B**)?

c Using this section, and pages 12–13, list the ways in which Hitler had broken the Versailles Treaty by 1939.

2 Fill in a table like the one below, for each of the events in **L**.

Date	Event	Hitler's aims	Reaction in Germany	Reaction abroad
1933	Germany left League	'equal treatment'		92% vote in plebiscite

3 How successful was Hitler's foreign policy in the 1930s?

20 War

The German invasion of Poland led Britain and France to declare war on Germany. At first the German Army was very successful. By 1942 the Germans had gained control over much of Europe (see map at the back of the book). Charts **A–C** show the main campaigns in which Germany was involved. (See also *The Second World War* in this series.)

A Blitzkrieg

1939	**Poland**
	1–18 September – Germans used *Blitzkrieg* (lightning war) – speed, surprise attacks, tanks, planes – to destroy the Polish army.
	Britain and France demanded that Germany withdraw. Germany refused so they declared war. Germany took Danzig and regained land lost after World War I. Hitler made Poland a slave nation. SS Commandos *(Einsatzgruppen)* followed the German Army and shot thousands of Polish people.
1940	**Denmark and Norway**
	April – the Germans invaded Denmark and Norway.
1940	**The Western Front**
	10 May – Germans launched Blitzkrieg on the Netherlands.
	15 May – Netherlands surrendered.
	28 May – Belgium surrendered. British and French troops forced to retreat from Dunkirk beaches.
	5–24 June – Germans advanced into France.
	14 June – Germans took Paris.
	22 June – French signed ceasefire (armistice) at the place where Germany had surrendered in 1918. Hitler divided France into two parts, one occupied by Nazis, one controlled by France.
1940–1	**Battle of Britain**
	Germans launched air attacks against Britain, and bombed British cities, including London, Coventry and Plymouth (the Blitz). But the Luftwaffe (airforce) failed to defeat RAF fighters in southern England. Hitler postponed 'Operation Sea Lion' plan to invade Britain.

1941	*22 June* – Hitler launched 'Operation Barbarossa' – invasion of Russia. The Russians were taken by surprise. Germans viewed the Russians as 'subhuman'. SS squads shot many, others sent to detention camps.
	October – Germans approached Moscow.
	December – Germans forced to retreat. Hitler took over supreme command of the army.
1942	*Summer* – Germans mounted another offensive.
	September–November – Germans took most of Stalingrad.
	November – Russians encircled German forces.
1943	*February* – German commander, Von Paulus, and 100 000 men surrendered at Stalingrad.

B War in Russia (the Eastern Front)

1941	*January* – Hitler set up the Africa corps under Rommel.
	April – Germans defeated Greece and Yugoslavia.
	May–June – Germans occupied Crete.
1942	*June* – German/Italian forces crossed into Egypt.
	30 June – Germans and Italians advanced to El Alamein.
	4 November – Allies defeated Rommel at El Alamein.

C North Africa and the Balkans

??????????????????

1 'to Hitler, the Russian campaign was not a luxury; it was the be-all and end-all of Nazism'

(Hugh Trevor-Roper, a British historian)

Use the evidence here and in chapter 12 to explain what this statement means. Do you agree? Why?

2 Use **B**, **D–F** to write a letter from a German soldier to his family, describing conditions in Russia. How might **E** and **F** be biased?

What went wrong?

Chart **B** describes the German campaign against Russia 1941–43. On 3 July 1941, German General Halder wrote in his diary:

❝*The Russian campaign has been won in the space of two weeks.*❞ (D)

But by 11 August things looked different:

❝*We reckoned with about 200 enemy divisions. Now we have already counted 360. The time factor favours them, as they are near their own resources, whereas we are moving farther and farther away from ours. And so our troops, spread over an immense front line, without any depth, are subjected to the enemy's incessant attacks.*❞ (E)

F shows the sort of conditions the Germans had to face in the winter.

F German soldiers on the Eastern Front

Motives

Jumbled up below are some of the things that Hitler did, and possible reasons for his actions. First, use the timecharts (A–C) to put the events in the order they happened. Then link each of the actions with a reason.

For example	Action	Reason
	9	f

Some historians say that Hitler attacked Greece and Yugoslavia to reduce the threat from Britain and to provide bases for an attack on Russia.

Action	Reason
1 Attacked Russia.	**a** Wanted to support Italy and weaken Britain in all areas of the world.
2 Planned to invade Britain.	**b** Wanted to defeat Russia at all costs.
3 Invaded Norway.	**c** Wanted to prevent USA from helping Britain in the West, so he could concentrate on Russia.
4 Rejected peace moves from Stalin in 1942/3.	**d** Needed to defeat all western countries before attacking Russia.
5 Joined Japan in declaring war on USA, December 1941.	**e** To destroy Bolshevism and provide 'Lebensraum' (living space).
6 Invaded Poland.	**f** To reduce the threat from Britain and provide bases for an attack on Russia.
7 Fought the Battle of Britain.	**g** Wanted bases in North Atlantic and to protect iron ore supplies.
8 Sent army under Rommel to North Africa.	**h** Wanted 'Lebensraum'.
9 Attacked Greece and Yugoslavia.	**i** Needed air superiority before he could launch attack by sea.

41

21 Life in Wartime Germany

Mathilde Wolff-Mönckeberg wrote a diary of her experiences while living in Hamburg during the Second World War. She wrote it for her children who were abroad. The diary is important evidence on what happened to people at this time. Mathilde described her feelings in 1939:

When on 1 September 1939 war broke out, your stepfather Wolff and I and all those nearest to us were in absolute despair. We were convinced that immediate and total annihilation would follow . . . **(A)**

Instead of destruction, Germans heard of victory after victory. Mathilde was surprised by the success of the German Army. In mid-1940 she wrote:

The progress of our troops is fantastic, they are driving a wedge right into the massive army of French, British and Belgian soldiers. **(B)**

In her entry for October 1940 she described how things were difficult for some people, like a friend whose husband was called up.

They have no children and she just cannot manage without him. And what sort of existence do she and many others lead? Rations for a single person are pathetic: 60 grammes of semolina and oats, 125 grammes of butter per week, 1 pound of meat and sausage per month. For this she has to queue for hours, and there is no one at home in her icy flat to make her a meal. She has to face the rest of the day in frozen silence. **(C)**

Many Germans were surprised at the attack on the USSR, but were told that all was set for another quick victory. The Nazi Party encouraged people to collect winter clothes for the troops on the Russian front. The mood changed when the government announced the defeat at Stalingrad. The Nazi intelligence service (SD) reported on 28 January 1943:

The whole nation is deeply shaken . . . people ask above all why Stalingrad was not evacuated or relieved, and how it was possible, only a few months ago, to describe the military situation as secure . . . the nation is urgently waiting for a speech by the Führer (Hitler) on 30 January . . . **(D)**

On 18 February Goebbels spoke to 10 000 people at the Berlin Sports Palace. All radio stations broadcast his speech. He could hardly make himself heard, as the crowd answered each of his questions with a single roar of approval.

Do you believe with the Führer and with us in the final total victory of the German people?

And are the German people determined, if the Führer orders it, to work 10, 12 and if necessary, 14 and 16 hours a day and to give your utmost for victory?

The English say that the German people are resisting the total war measures of the government. (Cries of Never! Never! Never!)

I ask you: Do you want total war? The nation is ready for anything. The Führer has given his orders, we will follow him . . . **(E)**

Total war meant an all-out effort by everyone to win the war. Mathilde wrote in her diary on 2 March 1943:

How different the atmosphere is from that of the first war year when at the slightest provocation red Nazi flags were flown, drums were beaten on the radio announcing victory. Since the defeat at Stalingrad and the realisation of total war, all is grey and still and on 14 August . . . Goebbels declared total war to all at home. Everyone was called up, even women up to 50 years old, and mere boys had to do anti-aircraft duties. **(F)**

The SD reported:

A large section of the nation cannot imagine how the war will end, and the telling of vulgar jokes against the state, even about the Führer himself, has increased considerably since Stalingrad. **(G)**

In 1943 the Allies bombed German towns more heavily (see **H**). This increased the problems for the government. The bombing made some people more determined to fight. The government stressed that unless Germany won the Communists would take over. Mathilde described one of the many raids on Hamburg in her diary. She remembered the raid on 24 July 1943:

H Bombs dropped on Germany and Britain 1940–45
(in tons)

	On Germany	On Britain
1940	10 000	36 844
1941	30 000	21 858
1942	40 000	3 260
1943	120 000	2 298
1944	650 000	9 151
1945	500 000	761

Hitler had hoped for a short war. German industry was not ready for a long struggle. In 1942 Hitler put Albert Speer in charge of organising supplies for the army. Speer set about bringing raw materials from the countries which Germany had invaded, but he was faced with a shortage of workers. They had to be found from elsewhere (**L**). Workers were brought to Germany from the occupied countries, and after the announcement of 'total war' women were brought into the factories.

	1939	1940	1941	1942	1943	1944
Germans (men + women)	39.1	34.8	33.1	31.3	30.3	28.4
Women	14.6	14.4	14.1	14.4	14.8	14.9
Foreign workers, prisoners of war	0.3	1.2	3.0	4.1	6.3	7.1
Conscripts in army	1.4	5.7	7.4	9.4	11.2	13.0

L Workers in Germany 1939–44

K Survivors rescued from the wreckage after an Allied bombing raid on Mannheim

❝ *Shortly before 1 am the air-raid warning goes. As always we dress in a hurry, but before we even reach the shelter a thunderstorm of noise explodes above us. It doesn't stop for even a second. The house shakes, the windows tremble. For two whole hours this ear-splitting terror goes on and all you can see is fire. No one speaks during the night of Tuesday. Wednesday there was yet another terror attack . . . We sat with wet towels over nose and mouth and the noise from one direct hit after another was such that the entire house shook and rattled, plaster spilling from the walls and glass splintering from the windows. Never have I felt the nearness of death so intensely. The following morning Maria reported that all women and children had to be evacuated from the city within six hours. There was no gas, no electricity, not a drop of water, neither the lift nor the telephone was working. It is hard to imagine the panic and chaos.* ❞ (**J**)

??????????????????

1 a Use the table below and the evidence on these pages to summarise Mathilde's changing feelings over the war years. Number each source on a scale from 1–5: 1 = hopeful; 5 = despairing.

Source	Date	Feelings	Reason
A			
B			
C			
F			
J			

b Which of sources **D–F** is most useful? Explain the reason for your choice.

2 Design a poster for the Nazi government to try to boost morale in 1943. (Include the words victory; Communists; Lebensraum; Jews . . .)

3 a Why was there a shortage of labour in Nazi Germany (**L**)?
b How was this problem solved?
c Why was Hitler reluctant to employ women?

4 How did the war change the life of a family in Germany? Mention food, work, bombing . . . Use as much of the material in this section as you can.

22 The 'Final Solution'

In the late 1930s Nazi policy towards the Jews (see pages 32–33) became more extreme. Nazi leaders wished to rid Germany of Jews. Their first 'solution' was to send Jews to other countries. Hitler put Reinhard Heydrich in charge of this. Hitler spoke out more and more against the Jewish race. On 30 January 1939 he promised the 'destruction of the Jews in Europe'.

When war broke out in 1939 it became more difficult to send Jews to other countries. With the takeover of Austria, Czechoslovakia and Poland there were now 3.5 million more Jews under Nazi control. The SS commanders shot many Jews as the German army advanced through Poland. Others were used as forced labour. Heydrich gave up the idea of getting the Jews to live abroad. He ordered Jews to be moved from Germany to Poland.

Hitler blamed the Jews for Communism. After invading the USSR in May 1941 he put new energy into his plans for destroying the Jews. On 31 July 1941 Göring sent an order to Heydrich:

❝*I hereby charge you with making all necessary preparations with regard to organisational, technical, and financial matters for bringing about a final solution of the Jewish question within the German sphere of influence in Europe.*❞
(A)

From October 1941 large numbers of Jews were sent from Germany to particular parts of towns (*ghettoes*) in places like Lodz, Warsaw, Minsk and Riga. **B** shows Nazi concentration camps. In December 1941 the SS opened an *extermination camp* at Chelmno in Poland. More were opened in 1942. The largest was Auschwitz-Birkenau. By the end of the war, the Nazis had killed an estimated six million Jews.

Auschwitz

Rudolf Höss was the commandant of Auschwitz. At the end of the war he remembered a conversation with Himmler (leader of the SS) in 1941. Himmler said:

❝*The Führer has ordered that the Jewish question be solved once and for all, and that we the SS are to carry out the order. I have earmarked Auschwitz for this purpose because of its good position as regards communications and because the area can easily be isolated and camouflaged.*❞ **(C)**

The SS brought Jewish people from all over Europe to Auschwitz. (They also transported gypsies, Russians,

B Nazi concentration camps in Europe

Poles and other groups.) The Jews were told that they would be 'resettled'. Some even had to buy their own train tickets. They travelled to Auschwitz in goods coaches, without food or toilets. At the railway ramp in Birkenau they went through a selection process. Höss described what happened:

❝*The vans were unloaded one after the other. After depositing their baggage, the Jews had to pass individually in front of an SS doctor. Those considered capable of work were taken into the camp in small groups.*❞ **(D)**

The others were sent to the gas chambers.

Wieslaw Kielar was arrested by the Gestapo in May 1940. He was taken to Auschwitz:

❝*We were led into the basement where all our personal belongings were taken away; this included removal of hair from every part of our body, followed by a bath in ice-cold* water. *We were handed a cardboard tab with a number which was to replace our names from now on. My number was 290.* **"** (**E**)

Later the number was tattooed onto the prisoner. Kielar wrote:

" *This is my third day in the camp. Three slices of bread, three bowls of soup, three small pieces of bacon, a few bruises, dozens of kicks, the guards outdid each other in inventing ever-new tortures.* **"** (**F**)

The guards organised endless roll-calls. The roll-call of 6 July 1940 lasted from 7 pm, through the night, until 2 pm the next day. One of the jobs that the prisoners were made to do was build parts of the camp. A former prisoner remembers.

" *Work consisted of unloading heavy loads, of pulling down the barracks. Everything had to be done double quick, should anyone fall down exhausted, he would be beaten and kicked.* **"** (**G**)

Another prisoner described living conditions.

" *The block was filled to capacity by four rows of low berths, looking like a three-tier chicken house. It was always damp and cold inside . . . The stink, thirst and hunger made sleep impossible.* **"** (**H**)

J is a painting done by a prisoner at Auschwitz-Birkenau.

Many prisoners died from exhaustion, starvation and disease. Others were tortured by the guards and shot for disobeying rules. Medical experiments killed some prisoners. Between three and four million people died at Auschwitz. Höss described how most of these were killed.

" *The Camp Commandant at Treblinka* (another camp) *told me that he had liquidated 80 000 in six months. He used*

J An execution at Auschwitz, painted by a prisoner there

monoxide gas and I did not think that his methods were very efficient. So when I set up the extermination building at Auschwitz, I used cyclon B. It took from 3 to 15 minutes to kill the people in the death chamber. We knew the people were dead because their screaming stopped . . . After the bodies were removed our special squads took off the rings and extracted the gold from the teeth of the corpses.* **"** (**K**)

At the end of the war the Nazis tried to destroy the evidence of their crimes by blowing up the camp. The remains of Auschwitz-Birkenau are now a museum. L is a poem inspired by the museum.

L 'The Pigtail'

When all the women in the transport
had their heads shaved
four workmen with brooms made of birch twigs
swept up
and gathered up the hair

Behind clean glass
the stiff hair lies
of those suffocated in gas chambers
there are pins and combs
in this hair

The hair is not shot through with light
is not parted by the breeze
is not touched by any hand
or rain or lips

In huge chests
clouds of dry hair
of those suffocated
and a faded plait
a pigtail with a ribbon
pulled at school
by naughty boys

The museum, Auschwitz, 1948
T. Rózewicz

??????????????

1 a What plans did Nazi leaders have for the Jews in the 1930s?
b In your own words, say what Göring asked Heydrich to do in July 1941 (**A**).
c Why did Himmler choose Auschwitz as a site for his extermination camp (**C**)?
d Höss said **D** and **K** at his trial after the war. How do you think he felt about what he had done?

2 Look at **B**. In which country did most Jews die? Put the other countries in order, according to the numbers of Jews killed?

3 Which piece of evidence (**D–L**) do you find most helpful in understanding what it was like to be at Auschwitz? Give reasons for your answer.

4 Describe in detail how and why Nazi policies towards the Jews became more extreme after 1939.

23 Resistance

‘ . . . I now want to mention, quite openly before you all, a difficult subject. Among ourselves it can be openly discussed but it must never be mentioned in public. I mean the . . . extermination of the Jewish people. Any member of the Party will tell you "the Jews will be exterminated. It's quite clear, part of our programme . . ." And then they all come, those 80 million honest Germans and each has his "good" Jew, all the others are swine but this Jew is a first class fellow. But not one of them has seen it done, seen it through to the very end. Most of you will know what it means to have a hundred corpses lying there, or 500 or a 1000. To have seen this through and — except for a few exceptions due to human weakness — to have remained decent, this has made us hard and is a page of glory in our history which never has been and never will be mentioned. ’ (A)

This was from a speech by Heinrich Himmler to SS generals in Poland on 10 October 1943. The extermination of the Jews was not a secret. How many people knew exactly what was going on? When a friend told Albert Speer not to go to visit a concentration camp Speer said:

‘I did not query him. I did not query Himmler, I did not query Hitler, I did not speak with personal friends. I did not investigate — for I did not want to know what was happening there. ’ (B)

After the war many Germans said the same thing, that they didn't know what was going on. The killings were done secretly but many people knew what was happening. Soldiers returning from the front told their families about what they had seen. German Jews saw their relatives disappear. Perhaps, like Speer, some people did not *want* to know what was going on.

Many Germans supported Hitler. After all, he had created jobs for people and broken the hated Treaty of Versailles. But there was some opposition, from the following groups:

Communists

The German Communist party had 300 000 members in 1933. Hitler arrested many of them, others went into hiding or abroad. Those who stayed in Germany tried to organise strikes or get people to stand up against the Nazis. They stuck up slogans in the street, like C:

‘Only the overthrow of Hitler will bring freedom and bread! ’ (C) (Freedom)

Communists wanted a revolution in Germany similar to the one in Russia in 1917.

Social Democrats

The Social Democrats were the second largest party in the March 1933 election. This was remarkable since the Nazis had arrested many of the members and banned their newspapers. They voted against the Enabling Act (see page 28) and hoped that the Nazi government would collapse. When the Nazis banned the Social Democrats many of their leaders went abroad. Those who stayed in Germany printed illegal newspapers and pamphlets. Many were caught and arrested.

Youth

Some young people organised themselves against the Nazis. The most famous of these was the *White Rose* group. Hans and Sophie Scholl were the leaders of the White Rose. They were students at Munich University and worked with their Professor and others to produce pamphlets telling people about Nazi crimes. The Nazis arrested and executed them.

Churches

The Nazis tried to get control of the Protestant Church by using a group called the 'German Christians'. To get control of Catholics the Nazis made an agreement (*Concordat*) with the Catholic Church. Some churchmen spoke out against the Nazis. In a sermon on 20 July 1941 the Bishop of Münster said:

‘Become hard! Be firm! Remain upright! It may be that obedience to God and loyalty to your conscience will cost you or me life, freedom or home. But better to die than to sin! ’ (D)

The Nazis could not stop the Bishop, as Goebbels said:

‘If anything were done against the Bishop, the population of Münster could be regarded as lost to the war effort. ’ (E)

When the Bishop of Münster attacked the Nazi programme of *euthanasia* (killing old and ill people) it was halted. The Nazis put thousands of churchmen into concentration camps.

Conservatives

Some people who had supported the Nazis and worked in important jobs in the Nazi government became worried by Hitler's policies. Carl Goerdeler resigned from his post as Mayor of Leipzig as a protest against Hitler's anti-Jewish policy. Ulrich von Hassell was German ambassador in Rome from 1932 until 1937. He was against Hitler's foreign policy. He wrote in his diary for 19 October 1939:

Among well-informed people in Berlin I noticed a good deal of despair . . . The principal sentiments are: the conviction that the war cannot be won militarily; a realisation of the highly dangerous economic situation, the feeling of being led by criminal adventurers, and the disgrace that has sullied the German name through the conduct of the war in Poland; namely, the brutal use of air power and the shocking bestialities of the SS, especially toward the Jews . . . When people use their revolvers to shoot down a group of Jews herded into a synagogue, one is filled with shame. (F)

The Army

In the summer of 1938 some army officers planned to take power from Hitler. On 16 July 1938 General Beck wrote that the action against Czechoslovakia:

will automatically lead to a European or World War. Such a war will in all probability end not only in a military but also in a general catastrope for Germany. (G)

Hitler's takeover of Czechoslovakia was highly successful. The officers abandoned their plot. To continue an attack on Hitler would have been unpopular and seemed unpatriotic at this time.

After the defeats of Stalingrad and in North Africa (see pages 40–41) army leaders and some of the conservatives plotted again. When they heard the news that the Allies had landed in Normandy they decided to take urgent action:

The assassination (of Hitler) must be attempted at any cost. We must prove to the world and to future generations that the men of the German Resistance dared to take the decisive step and to risk their lives on it. (H)

On 20 July 1944 Hitler held a meeting at his 'Wolf's Lair' headquarters in East Prussia. One of the conspirators, Claus von Stauffenberg arrived with a bomb in his briefcase. He sat down near Hitler and put the case under the table. He set the fuse and then left the room

J Hitler's meeting room after the unsuccessful attempt to kill him

to make a phone call. At 12.42 pm an explosion shattered the room (J). Hitler was covered in dust and injured but he was alive. The heavy table had saved his life.

In the meantime Stauffenberg had gone to Berlin and, thinking that Hitler was dead, made plans to take over the government. The Gestapo arrested and shot Stauffenberg. A People's Court passed the death sentence on 200 people. Goerdeler and Von Hassell were among those executed.

???????????????

1 a Why did Himmler want the extermination of the Jews kept secret (**A**)?
b What methods does he use in speech **A** to get the support of his audience?
c What reason does Speer give for not asking questions (**B**)?
d Why did many Germans support Hitler?

2 a How would you check the accuracy of Von Hassell's view in **F**?
b Why might photograph **J** have been taken?

3 a Why did some army leaders oppose Hitler: in 1938 (see **G**); in 1944 (see **H**)?
b In what ways had their position changed by 1944?

4 List the different groups which resisted Hitler. What difficulties did they have to face? How much did the various groups have in common? Which was the most effective in opposition to Hitler?

24 The Collapse of Germany

Some of the German army leaders were worried about what would happen to Germany if it was defeated. Hitler still believed victory was possible. Goebbels remembered Hitler saying to a meeting of Party leaders in May 1943:

❝The Reich will be the master of all Europe. We shall yet have to engage in many fights, but these will undoubtedly lead to magnificent victories. Thereafter the way to world domination is practically certain. To dominate Europe will be to assume the leadership of the world. We must never have the slightest doubt of victory. The Führer is firmly determined in all circumstances to fight this fight through to the end.❞ (A)

Morale in Germany was still remarkably high, but life was getting difficult. The call-up age for the army was lowered to 16½ and a home guard or *Volkssturm* was started. The Russian army was advancing in the East and the Allies in the West (B). Rommel pointed out the difficulties the troops in the West faced on 15 July 1944:

B The Allied advance on Germany 1944–45

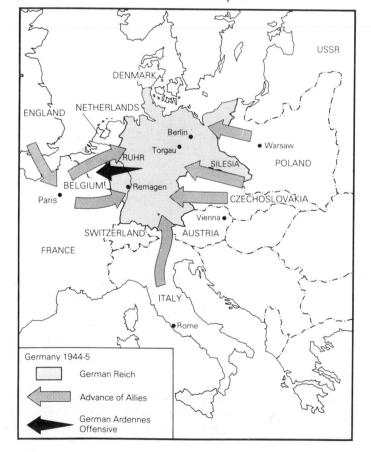

Germany 1944-5

▭ German Reich

⬅ Advance of Allies

⬅ German Ardennes Offensive

❝The situation on the Normandy Front is becoming more difficult every day. As a result of the fierceness of the fighting, the extremely large amounts of material used by the enemy, particularly in terms of artillery and tanks, and the impact of the enemy air force which is in absolute control of the combat area, our own losses are so high that they seriously reduce the operational effectiveness of our divisions. The supply situation is also difficult, because of the destruction of the railway network and the vulnerability of the roads to air attack up to 150 kilometres behind the front . . . The enemy front line units, on the other hand, receive new forces and supplies of war material every day.❞ (C)

Rommel advised Hitler to negotiate with the Allies. Hitler refused, and in December ordered a counter-attack in the Ardennes. This failed. Bombing of German towns increased, and life for ordinary people became increasingly difficult.

In the spring of 1945 a Berlin woman filled three exercise books with notes about her experiences. She wrote most of these notes during air-raids. She described life in the cellars of Berlin:

❝The cellar tribe in this house is convinced that its cave is the safest. There's nothing stranger than a strange cellar. I have belonged to this one for more than three months and I feel a stranger in it. Each cellar has its own taboos, its own fads. In my old cellar they had a rage for extinguishing water, everywhere one bumped into buckets, jugs, pots and barrels filled with a muddy brew. It didn't prevent the house from burning like a torch. The whole lot would have been as much use as spitting.❞ (D)

In Berlin the commanding officer issued an order for the defence of the city on 9 March 1945:

❝The capital will be defended to the last man and the last bullet. It is a condition for the successful defence of Berlin that: every building; every house; every floor; every hedge; every shell-crater; be defended to the utmost.❞ (E)

F shows this desperate fight. Soon even Hitler had to recognise that Germany would be defeated. The Allies were advancing on all sides (see G). On 19 March 1945 Hitler issued his 'destruction order':

❝Every possibility of doing lasting damage to the striking power of the enemy must be taken advantage of. I therefore order: All military, transport, communication, industrial and supply installations as well as equipment within the Reich which the enemy might use for the continuation of his struggle now or in the future must be destroyed. **)** (**H**)

Hitler decided to stay in Berlin and, as the Russian troops closed in on the city, Hitler wrote his Political Testament:

(*29 April 1945 4 am. More than 30 years have now passed since in 1914 I made my modest contribution as a volunteer in the First World War that was forced upon the Reich.*

It is untrue that I or anyone else in Germany wanted the war in 1939. It was devised and started by those international statesmen who were either of Jewish descent or worked for Jewish interest. **)** (**J**)

Historian Alan Bullock has described what happened to Hitler:

(*Hitler was lying on the sofa, which was soaked in blood, he had shot himself through the mouth. On his right-hand side lay Eva Braun, Hitler's wife, also dead: she had swallowed poison. The time was 3.30 pm on the afternoon of Monday 30 April 1945, 10 days after Hitler's 56th birthday. The bodies were laid in a shallow depression of sandy soil close to the porch. Picking up the fire cans of petrol Hitler's SS adjutant poured the contents over the two corpses and set fire to them with a lighted rag.* **)** (**K**)

Hitler had appointed Admiral Dönitz, Commander in Chief of the Navy, as President of the Reich. On 7 May 1945 the Germany army surrendered to USA, GB, USSR and France.

F Civilians building barricades to defend Hitler's headquarters in Berlin

G Timechart: January – May 1945

1945	East	West
January	Soviet offensive into Poland. Soviets occupied Silesia.	Allied offensive in Ardennes.
February		Allies took left bank of Rhine.
March		Americans took Remagen. British advanced in North Germany. Americans reached River Elbe.
April	Soviets advanced from Rivers Oder + Neisse. Soviets encircled Berlin.	Allies took Ruhr. Americans + French advanced in south.
	American and Soviet troops met at Torgau.	
	Hitler killed himself.	
May	Surrender of Berlin.	
	Unconditional surrender of German forces.	

??????????????????

1 a What aim did Hitler have in 1943 (**A**)?
  b What problems faced Germany in 1944 (**B**, **C**)?

2 Using **D**, **E** and **F**, make up interviews with a woman, a soldier and an army officer in Berlin in Spring 1945. What do they tell you about life in the city, their feelings about the war . . .?

3 a How reliable are **J** and **K** as historical evidence?
  b What do they tell us about the collapse of Germany and Hitler?

4 What factors led to the collapse of Germany in 1945? Why did Hitler fail to achieve his aims?

25 Problems of the Peace

A The ruins of Dresden after the war

1945. Germany's cities were in ruins (**A**). Families had fled from their homes. Ex-soldiers came back to a society in chaos. The writer Wolfgang Borchert was born in Hamburg in 1921. In 1941 he fought in the German army on the Russian front. **B** is an extract from one of his stories:

❝ *When the war was over, the soldier came home. But he had no bread. Then he saw a man who had. He killed him. "You mustn't kill people, you know," said the judge. "Why not?" asked the soldier.* ❞ (**B**)

C is from the beginning of Borchert's play *The Man Outside*, which he wrote at the end of the war.

❝ *A man comes to Germany.*

He's been away for a long time, this man. A very long time. Perhaps too long. He has waited outside in the cold for a thousand days. And as entrance fee he's paid with his knee-cap. And after waiting outside in the cold for a thousand nights, he actually − finally − comes home.

A man comes to Germany.

. . . One of the many who comes home − and then doesn't come home, because there's no home for them any more. ❞ (**C**)

---

1 8.3 million Germans had died in the war.
2 Bombing had made 7.5 million people homeless.
3 3.6 million houses had been destroyed.
4 People in Eastern Europe had moved west to avoid the advancing Russian army. There were 12 million refugees.
5 In Cologne only 12% of children had the normal weight for their age.
6 Many people had no jobs.
7 Trains, buses and trams were not running.
8 Shops were empty. Many things could only be bought on the black market.
9 In 1946 German industry produced only 25% of what it produced in 1936.

D Problems facing Germany in 1945

Chart **D** shows some of the problems which faced Germany in 1945. At the end of the war Britain, Russia and America had occupied Germany. Now they had to decide what to do about these problems. The Allied leaders met at peace conferences at Yalta and Potsdam to decide Germany's fate.

The Yalta Conference

In February 1945 Roosevelt (USA), Churchill (GB) and Stalin (USSR) met at Yalta in the Crimea. Among other things, they decided that:

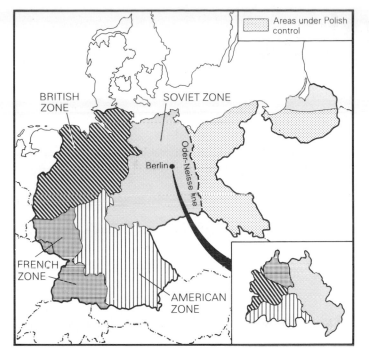

E How Germany was divided

They must get rid of Nazism from Germany after the war (*denazification*).

They should divide Germany into Russian, British and American zones. (They later added a French zone.)

Berlin was too important to be occupied by just one country (see map **E**).

The leaders should continue to meet together to discuss problems and plans for the future.

In May 1945 the Germans surrendered. The Allied leaders met again at Potsdam near Berlin, from 16 July to 2 August.

The Potsdam Conference

Truman represented the USA, Stalin the USSR and Churchill and Attlee Great Britain. Each of the Allies had its own ideas about the future of Germany:

America was afraid that Russia would move towards the West. It saw Germany as a barrier which would stop the Russians from expanding. Truman wrote:

❝*At my forthcoming meeting with Churchill and Stalin I intended to call for a centralised Allied control (German) government. I was opposed to the breaking-up of Germany into several Allied segments.*❞ **(F)**

France had been invaded by Germany in two World Wars. On 7 August 1945 the French Foreign Minister said:

❝*The French Government is particularly anxious about the*

re-establishment of political parties serving the whole of Germany.❞ **(G)**

Britain, like America, was afraid of Russian expansion. On 22 February 1944 Churchill said to the House of Commons:

❝*Unconditional surrender means that the victors have a free hand. It does not mean that they are entitled to behave in a barbarous manner, nor that they wish to blot out Germany from among the nations of Europe.*❞ **(H)**

Russia had lost 20 million people in the war, and did not want Germany to become strong again. Russia wanted to keep the Americans as far away as possible. On 9 May 1945 Stalin said:

❝*The Soviet Union celebrates the victory, even if she is not ready to break up or destroy Germany.*❞ **(J)**

K shows what the Allies agreed at the Potsdam talks.

One of the ways the Allies tried to stamp out Nazism was by holding trials of Nazi war criminals. Between 1945 and 1947, there were 13 trials of major war criminals at Nuremberg. In 1946, 10 of the accused were executed. The chief Nazi on trial, Hermann Göring, was condemned to death, but committed suicide before he could be executed. Other Nazi leaders were jailed.

K Terms agreed at the Potsdam talks

1 Germany should not have a central government.
2 They should treat Germany as a 'single economic unit'.
3 Poland and the USSR should run the areas they had occupied (the Eastern Territories).
4 Germans living in the Eastern Territories, Poland, Czechoslovakia and Hungary should be moved to Germany.
5 The Allies could take property from their respective zones as reparations.
6 They were to get rid of Nazism.
7 Germany was not allowed to have an army.

??????????????????

1 a What is Borchert saying about war in **B**?
  b Do you agree with the message of **B**?
  c How useful are **B** and **C** to the historian studying Germany in 1945?

2 Draw four columns headed: USA; USSR; Britain; France. Under each heading, list the demands of that country in 1945. Your list should reflect what each country would like done with Germany.

3 What problems did the Allies have to deal with when they occupied Germany in 1945? How far did they succeed in dealing with these problems? Mention: economic problems; the future shape of Germany; denazification.

26 Germany Divided

A Russian soldiers raise the Soviet flag above the Reichstag in Berlin

C The division of Berlin

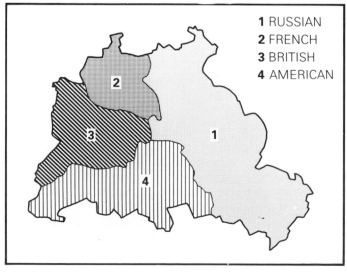

1 RUSSIAN
2 FRENCH
3 BRITISH
4 AMERICAN

Berlin

On 30 April 1945 the Soviet flag was hoisted on the *Reichstag* (the parliament building in Berlin) (see **A**). On 2 May Soviet troops completed their conquest of Berlin. Soviet Marshal Zhukov described later what he found there:

❛*Traffic in the city had come to a standstill, more than one third of all the underground stations had been flooded. The Nazi troops had blown up 225 bridges. The tram cars and overhead cables were almost totally destroyed. The streets were little more than a heap of rubble, especially in the city centre . . . power stations, gas and water works and the sewage disposal system were paralysed.*❜ **(B)**

The Allies had agreed at the peace conferences (see pages 50–51) that Berlin should be run by the four allied powers. Berlin was divided into American, French, British and Russian sectors (see map **C**). It was too important to be under the control of any one power. In July 1945 British, American and French troops arrived to occupy their sectors. The three western sectors of Berlin were an 'island' in the middle of the Soviet zone of Germany (see **E** on page 51).

From 1945 the Western and Soviet zones were run in their own ways. Out of these zones grew two new countries, East and West Germany.

Western Zones

At the end of May 1945 there was only enough food left for 60 days in the Western zones of Germany. Food had to be brought in if people were not to starve to death. Britain, France and America decided the only way of feeding Germany would be to get German farms and factories working again. Cartoon **D** shows a British view of this problem. The American Secretary of State said in September 1946:

❛*Germany is part of Europe and recovery in Europe, and particularly in the states adjoining Germany, will be slow indeed if Germany with her great resources of iron and coal is turned into a poorhouse.*❜ **(E)**

The British found that their zone was costing too much to run. So the British and Americans joined their zones in January 1947. The joint zone was called the Bi-zone.

American President Truman announced on 12 March 1947:

"IF WE DON'T LET HIM WORK, WHO'S GOING TO KEEP HIM!"

D A British view of the German problem

❛*I believe that it must be the policy of the United States to support free peoples who are resisting attempted subjugation by armed minorities or by outside pressures.*❜ **(F)**

This idea of giving help to countries which America's enemies wanted to take over was called the *Truman Doctrine*. George Marshall, the American Secretary of State, set out a plan to help Europe recover from the war. He said:

❛*It is logical that the United States should do whatever it is able to assist the return of normal economic health in the world, without which there can be no political stability and no assured peace.*❜ **(G)**

America said she would help countries if they agreed to a *European Recovery Programme* (ERP). In the Spring of 1948 the Western zones of Germany, along with 17 other European countries, joined the *Marshall Plan*. H is a poster advertising the Marshall Plan. Cartoon J is a Russian view of Western help to Germany. The USSR turned down America's offer of aid for the Eastern zone of Germany. An East German historian has written about the Marshall Plan:

❛*Goods, supplies and credits from the USA, with political and economic conditions attached to them were geared to the policy of the cold war, the aim being to help stabilize the weakened capitalist system in Europe and push back socialism. The USA and its allies had set course on the partitioning of Germany.*❜ **(K)**

H Poster in support of the Marshall Plan

The Western Allies soon found it difficult to work with the USSR. They suggested a new system of government for the Western zones. The USSR disagreed with this and on 20 March 1948 the Soviet representative walked out of the Allied Control Council. The Western Allies now worked more closely together. In the summer of 1948 the French joined their zone to the American and British zones. The Western zones were then called the Tri-zone.

Soviet zone

The food shortage in the Eastern zone was even worse than in the West. The USSR did not provide its zone with food and machines. It wanted to rebuild Russia first. Indeed, machinery was taken from Germany to rebuild Russian industry, which the war had destroyed. The Russians wanted to set up a communist state in their zone. They took over land belonging to Nazis, and broke up large estates into smaller parts. This land was given to farm labourers or Germans whom the Russians had moved into the Soviet zone from the East. In October 1945 the Russians took over the wealth of the German state.

Economic recovery was slower in the Soviet zone than the Western zones because: the USSR broke up industry and took reparations (for instance a third of the railway track was removed); the Western zones had more natural resources and heavy industry; the Eastern zones did not accept help from America.

Currency reform in the Western zones

From 1945–48 a huge rise in prices (*inflation*) made life hard in the Western zone. To stop the price rise and also stamp out the black market, the British, French and American authorities introduced a new currency in the Western zones on 20 June 1948. Everyone could get 40 Deutsche Mark (German Mark) or DM with another 20 DM two months later. (Supplies were restricted in order to prevent a 'rush' on the new currency.) The old 'Reichsmark' were exchanged for the new DM at the rate of 10 to 1. A German newspaper reported on the effects of this on 26 June 1948:

❝*The new German Mark works wonders . . . Now you can buy briefcases, brushes, thermos flasks, shoelaces, buttons, books, fire-proof saucepans, pans for electric cookers, penknives, needles . . .* ❞ **(L)**

The USSR complained about this currency reform, and on 23 June 1948 announced a new currency for its zone and for Berlin. The USSR wanted to control the whole of Berlin and have a say in what was going on in the Western zone. The Russian leader Stalin decided to act. Berlin was *blockaded* (see page 55). During the blockade, the German state in the Western zones set up a Parliamentary Council. This Council wrote the 'Basic Law' for the Western part of Germany. They called West Germany the *Federal Republic of Germany*.

How did people feel about the formation of the Federal Republic? Here are two views:

❝*And so the West German State was founded in complete disregard of the right of self-determination of the German people and in violation of the basic principles of the Potsdam agreement.* ❞ **(M)**

❝*On 23 May, the Basic Law was proclaimed and it came into effect at the day's end. Freedom in Germany had a new beginning.* ❞ **(N)**

In the Eastern zone the *German Democratic Republic* (GDR) was founded. There were now two Germanies.

J A Russian cartoon comment on plans to rebuild Germany

?????????????????

1 a Imagine you are a Soviet soldier in photograph **A**. Write a diary entry for 30 April 1945. Use **A** and **B** to describe what you saw and felt.

2 a Why was Berlin divided into four sectors (see **C**)?
b In what way were the British, American and French sectors an 'island'?

3 a What is happening in cartoon **J**? What does this suggest about the cartoonist's attitude towards the Marshall Plan?
b In what ways do **H** and **K** differ in their view of the Marshall Plan? How would you account for these differences?

4 Why did the Western Allies decide to help reconstruct German industry in 1945? Why did Russia adopt a different policy?

5 Describe the steps which led to the founding of the two German states, from 1945 to 1949.

27 Berlin Blockade

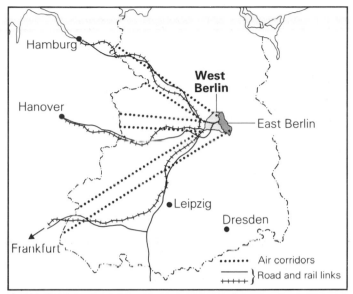

A Links between West Germany and West Berlin

20 June 1948	Currency reform in Western zones of Germany.
23	USSR announced currency reform for Soviet zone, and all of Berlin.
24	USSR blocked land routes between Berlin and the Western zones of Germany.
26	American Military Governor, Lucius D. Clay announced Western airlift.
12 May 1949	USSR lifted the blockade.

B Timechart: the Berlin Blockade

Between June 1948 and May 1949 the USSR blocked the land routes between West Berlin and the Western zones of Germany. So the Western powers flew in all the supplies that West Berlin needed. These included coal, food and raw materials for industry. **A** shows the routes to Berlin. **B** shows the main events of the blockade. (See also *The Great Power Conflict* in this series.)

How did these events affect people living in Berlin at the time? Klaus Scherff was there. He thinks that photographs like **C** give the wrong idea:

❝ *It is wrong to think that Berliners at that time sat on a pile of rubble, doing nothing apart from gazing at the planes overhead.* ❞ **(D)**

Despite terrible hardship, the Berliners refused to give in. They had to live on small amounts of food, and suffer power cuts. Some helped build new runways for the aircraft. **E** comes from Scherff's account of home life during the blockade.

❝ 6.15 *Father went to work.* 7.30 *Went to school.* 8.00 *Mother did the ironing, if there was electricity.* 9.00 *Mother went out to collect twigs for the evening fire . . . she stopped to listen to the news from the radio van. She bought a newspaper. The newspaper only had four pages. She queued at one shop for two hours. There was no meat on sale. Shopping consisted of dried beans, dried carrots, dried potatoes, powdered soup, powdered egg, dried plums, Canadian flour, synthetic coffee made from corn. She met a friend who had tried to go shopping in the Soviet Sector* (food was on sale there but West Berliners were not allowed to buy it) *. . . The friend was caught by an East Berlin policeman at the border . . . He confiscated the four pounds of potatoes and the flower pot that she had with her. On the way home Mother swapped a soap ration card for one for fat. She had had a successful day . . .* ❞
(E)

There were celebrations in West Berlin when the blockade ended in May 1949. The USSR had failed to take control over the whole of Berlin.

C

??????????????????

1 **a** Describe what is going on in **C**.
b Why might the people be pleased to see the plane?
c In what way might the photograph give us the wrong idea about the airlift (see **D**)?

2 In what ways were: the Berlin Blockade; the Allied airlift; important for the people of West Berlin?

28 West Germany

A The ruins of Munich in 1945

B A Munich square in the 1960s

Political parties	% vote in August 1949
Christian Democrats (CDU/CSU)	31.0
Social Democrats (SPD)	29.2
Free Democrats (FDP)	11.9
Communists (KPD)	5.7

(From 1953–82 there was no Communist MP as they failed to gain more than 5% of the vote)

System of government

This was laid down in the 'Basic Law'.
The President was given few powers (to avoid the mistakes of the Weimar Republic).
West Germany was divided into 10 *Länder* (states) with control over education, police etc.

Chancellors

Konrad Adenauer (CDU) 1949–63
Ludwig Erhard (CDU) 1963–66
Kurt Georg Kiesinger (CDU) 1966–69
Willy Brandt (SPD) 1969–74
Helmut Schmidt (SPD) 1974–82
Helmut Kohl (CDU) 1982–

C The Federal Republic of Germany

A shows Munich in 1945. B shows the same city in the 1960s. This section suggests how this West German city and the whole of West Germany were rebuilt after 1945.

West Germany, or the Federal Republic of Germany (*Bundesrepublik Deutschland*) was set up on 23 May 1949. The first elections to the Federal Parliament were held in August 1949. Konrad Adenauer, the leader of the winning Christian Democrat Party, was made Chancellor of the Federal Republic. C shows how the Republic was governed.

Adenauer's first problem was to help West Germany recover from the war. He made Ludwig Erhard Minister of Economics. Soon the rubble was cleared from towns, new houses were built (see **D**); there was more food;

there were more things in the shops; and more people were able to buy them (see **E**). All this happened so quickly, and was so surprising, that some people have called it an 'economic miracle'. **F** gives possible reasons for the 'miracle'.

A British journalist wrote in *The Financial Times* of 22 July 1952:

‘*Of course the Germans have many advantages. They regard work and not football pools as their national sport. They have virtually wiped out their internal debt. They have no*

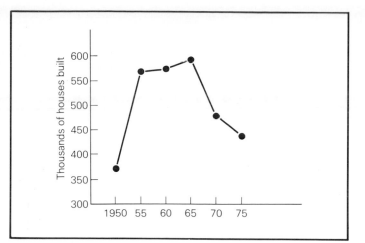

D New houses built 1950–75

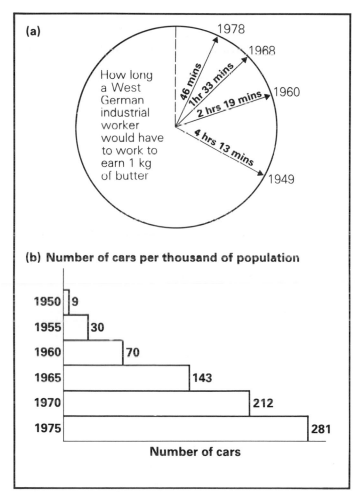

E The German 'economic miracle'

F Reasons for economic recovery

1 Many people wanted to buy German goods.
2 The Germans worked hard.
3 Since so much had been destroyed in the war, industry had to be almost totally modernised.
4 Help came from America under the Marshall Plan.
5 The currency was reformed (see page 54).

rearmament so far to bother them. On the other hand, they were, literally, eating out of their dustbins in 1945 and 1946. They have had occupation costs to bear. Their country was smashed in ruins. They have had this colossal influx of refugees. You can time their amazing recovery almost to the hour from the currency reform of 1948. (G)

By the end of the 1960s the West German economy was booming so rapidly that foreign workers had to be taken on. Foreign or 'guest' workers *(Gastarbeiter)* came from Turkey and other countries in southern Europe. They earned much more than they could in their home countries, but often faced discrimination.

During the 1960s and '70s the Federal Republic became strong and wealthy. By 1979, 40 per cent of West German families owned their own home. Most owned a car, fridge, washing machine and TV, as well as having some savings.

The West German government has however had to face some serious problems. Some groups, known as *Neo Nazis*, have tried to start up Nazi organisations again. Violent demonstrations and clashes with the police were a problem in the late 1960s and '70s – for example, there were demonstrations after police shot a student in June 1967, and again when Rudi Dutschke, a student leader, was attacked by a member of a right-wing group. Further clashes came in the 1970s when police evicted squatters from houses in Berlin, and during protests against the building of nuclear power stations in Germany.

Terrorism was a major problem for the West German government in the 1970s. The *Baader-Meinhof* group launched attacks on important politicians and industrialists. Most West Germans did not agree with the terrorists, but many became concerned about the brutal way the police dealt with terrorism.

??????????????

1 Imagine you are adviser to Konrad Adenauer in August 1949. List the main problems facing him. How would you suggest he dealt with them?

2 a What do **D** and **E** tell us about Germany's 'economic miracle'? What other information might be useful?
 b Put list **F** into your order of importance for causing the economic miracle. Give reasons for your order.

3 Compare photographs **A** and **B**, and describe the changes that have taken place. Use the evidence in this section, and any other information you can find, to explain why and how these changes happened.

29 East Germany

East Germany or the *German Democratic Republic* (GDR) was set up on 7 October 1949. The Socialist Unity Party (SED) under its communist leader Walter Ulbricht, ran the GDR.

The GDR faced many problems after 1949. In the early 1950s there were shortages of many goods in the shops. The government wanted industry to produce more, and workers demanded more money. Strikes broke out. Things got worse in 1952. The government said that workers would have to work longer hours for the same pay. They called this 'raising the work quotas'.

On 16 June 1953 building workers in East Berlin protested against the higher work quotas and marched to government offices. A crowd of 10 000 people gathered. A shows some of their demands. They called a general strike of all workers for 17 June 1953. On 17 June 300 000 workers in the GDR went on strike. Some of the demonstrations became violent. The Soviet army commander ordered in tanks to get rid of the crowds. A Swiss journalist described what happened in Berlin:

❝*We arrived just in time to see the Soviet tanks approach along the Leipziger Strasse. Suddenly shots come from the tanks, the first shots are in the air, the next are aimed at the demonstrators . . . the crowd moves back, we panic, people lie flat on the ground. We hear a scream, someone has been shot in the head. Ambulance men take him away, but he is already dead . . . the excited people get up and shake their fists shouting:*

"Aren't you ashamed to shoot at unarmed people?"❞ **(B)**

Photograph C shows demonstrations in the Potsdamer Platz in Berlin on 17 June 1953. 21 people were killed in these demonstrations.

The SED announced that they would keep the old work quotas, increase pensions and build more houses. Things quietened down. In the GDR the government criticised the workers and blamed the trouble on agitators from the West. The Secretary of the Writers' Union of GDR wrote on 20 June 1953:

❝*The Republic has looked after you well . . . you had no reason to fight . . . you were corrupted by your bad friends in the West. The Soviet Army and German People's Police look after you and the peace of the world. Aren't you ashamed of what you've done . . . you'll have to work hard if this is ever to be forgotten.*❞ **(D)**

The government of the GDR set about building up their country after these troubles. They reformed the

---

Solidarity Strike

The Building site . . . . in connection with the east Berlin building workers.

We demand:

1.) Full protection for the strike speakers.
2.) Free speech and freedom of the Press.
3.) Abolition of the norms.
4.) Wages corresponding to the prices in the German Democratic Republic. Revision of the whole price level for foodstuffs and consumer goods.
5.) Free elections for all Germany.
6.) Abolition of zonal boundaries.
7.) Withdrawal of all occupation troups.
8.) Abolition of the militarised People's Police.
9.) Immediate resumption of the 75% rebate on workmen's return tickets.
10.) Release of all political prisoners, even those sentenced to more than 3 years.
11.) Repatriation of all prisoners of war.
12.) Abolition of the „People's Controls".

Strike Committee of . . . . . building site

A The strike manifesto

C Potsdamer Platz 17 June 1953

E East Berlin

school system, and gave help to children of 'workers and peasants'. They built new universities and gave job training to pupils in schools. The SED took over land and farm machinery from private owners. They also took over factories. The State now owned most industries (*nationalisation*). By 1955, 82 per cent of industrial production was from state-owned industries. Everyone was promised a job, and by the 1970s the standard of living in the GDR was the highest in Eastern Europe.

Some people disliked the government or wanted a higher standard of living. At first, they left to live in West Germany. This became difficult after 1952, when the GDR government began to guard its frontier with West Germany more closely. But people began to use West Berlin as an 'escape route' to the West. The GDR government was worried about losing skilled people. So it built a wall between East and West Berlin in 1961 (see pages 62–63). It also strengthened the frontier with West Germany.

What is life like in the GDR? **E** shows East Berlin today. The singer Wolf Biermann described the GDR as:

An unattractive, fear-inspiring police state, which screws foreign currency out of its unhappy children and locks its communist critics either in or out, a state in whose coat of arms it is not the hammer and compass that are appropriate but the bludgeon and the muzzle. **(F)**

Biermann was banned. Erich Honecker, who replaced Ulbricht in 1971, said:

Biermann is currently betraying the basic ideas of Socialism. It is high time to take a stand against the spread of alien and dangerous ideas and inartistic junk. **(G)**

H was written by a British tourist visiting the GDR:

It was like going back twenty years. There weren't many cars on the road. Many of the buildings in the villages looked as if they hadn't been touched since the war. There were political slogans and red flags on many buildings. Many young people wore jeans, but the clothes had a strange outdated look about them. I suppose that sums the place up really. **(H)**

??????????????????

1 a Why were East German workers protesting in 1953?

b What can you see at points **1–3** in **C**?

c Use **B**, **C** and **D** to write a report on the events of 16/17 June 1953 for *either* a GDR or a Western newspaper.

2 a Look at **E**. What impression does it give of East Berlin?

b Does **H** give the same impression of life in GDR? How might you explain the differences?

c How useful is evidence like **E**, **F** and **H** to the historian?

3 Use the information in this and the previous section to compare life in the GDR and in the Federal Republic. Why can it be difficult to compare the two Germanies? Which would you prefer to live in? Why?

30 Across the Border

A shows the changing relations between East and West Germany from 1949 until the 1970s. **B** shows the number of people who left the GDR to live in the West between 1949 and 1961. Why did so many East Germans want to live in the West? Cartoon **C** may help you to answer this question.

In the 1960s relations between East and West Germany (see **A**) became increasingly difficult. The building of the Berlin Wall (see pages 62–63) made it harder to get to the West. The GDR further strengthened its border with the Federal Republic. **D** shows the border in 1980.

A Western visitor to the GDR in the 1970s described what it was like to leave the country after a visit there:

When you leave, searches sometimes include the X-raying of luggage. A long stick may be poked into the fuel tank to make sure that it hasn't been altered to provide hiding room for someone. The back seats are folded down for inspection, and the undercarriage examined with the aid of mirrors set in the road surface. It may take 20 minutes for such an inspection, 20 minutes' wait, and 20 minutes for passport control. In the summer, or on holidays, generally longer. **(E)**

B Number of refugees from East Germany (in thousands)

1949	1950	1951	1952	1953	1954	1955
75.8	197.8	161.4	171.3	331.3	184.2	252.9

1956	1957	1958	1959	1960	1961
279.2	261.6	204.0	143.9	199.2	207.0

The figures are for September to December of each year.

A Relations between East and West Germany 1949–72

1949 Berlin — East Germans leave for West

1952 East/West border strengthened. East Germans leave via West Berlin

1961 Berlin Wall built

West Germany	**1960s**	East Germany
'Eastern zone' is not a separate country		Citizens of GDR cannot visit West – with a few exceptions eg. politicians, sportsmen/women, singers
It is an unfriendly act for any country to recognise GDR – Hallstein doctrine		East Germans with relatives in West (a large number) could only see them on a few days each year

West Germany	**1970s**	East Germany
Let West Germans visit relatives in East! (Brandt)		Recognise GDR as a separate country! (Stoph)
	Meetings between Willy Brandt (Chancellor, FRG) and Willi Stoph (GDR leader), at: **Erfurt** (East Germany), 19 March 1970, **Kassel** (West Germany), 21 May 1970	
(Brandt's policy of negotiating with the East known as *Ostpolitik*)		

West Germany	**1972** Basic Treaty	East Germany
German Democratic Republic is independent		GDR pensioners can visit West. West Germans can visit GDR to see people and go on holiday.
There is one German nation. GDR is not a foreign country.		There are two German states. Federal Republic is a foreign country.

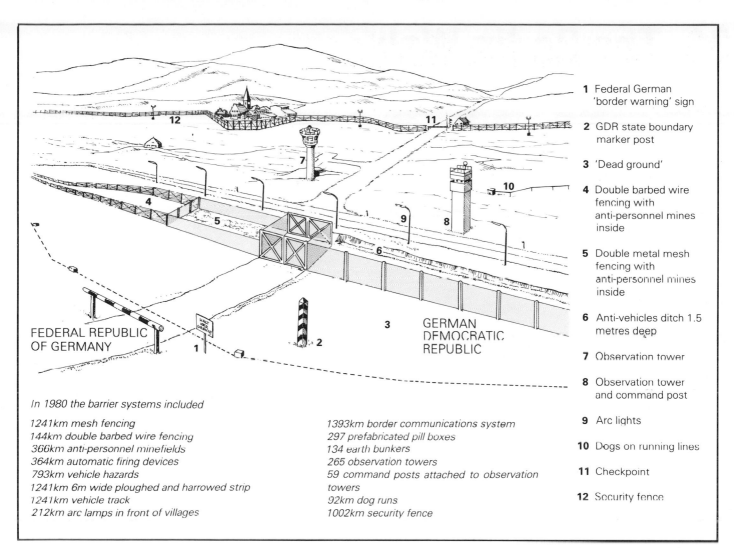

1 Federal German 'border warning' sign

2 GDR state boundary marker post

3 'Dead ground'

4 Double barbed wire fencing with anti-personnel mines inside

5 Double metal mesh fencing with anti-personnel mines inside

6 Anti-vehicles ditch 1.5 metres deep

7 Observation tower

8 Observation tower and command post

9 Arc lights

10 Dogs on running lines

11 Checkpoint

12 Security fence

FEDERAL REPUBLIC OF GERMANY

GERMAN DEMOCRATIC REPUBLIC

In 1980 the barrier systems included

1241km mesh fencing
144km double barbed wire fencing
366km anti-personnel minefields
364km automatic firing devices
793km vehicle hazards
1241km 6m wide ploughed and harrowed strip
1241km vehicle track
212km arc lamps in front of villages

1393km border communications system
297 prefabricated pill boxes
134 earth bunkers
265 observation towers
59 command posts attached to observation towers
92km dog runs
1002km security fence

D The border between East and West Germany

C 'Hey! There's someone behind you!' – a West German cartoon

??????????????????

1 a Look carefully at **D**. Explain the purpose of the defences at **1–5**.
b How would you plan to escape from East to West Germany through these defences?
c In what way is **D** biased?

2 a What does **C** suggest about the standard of living in East and West Germany?
b Why do you think the cartoonist wanted to point this out?
c What does the cartoon tell us about the West Germans' view of the East Germans?

3 Write an account of an interview with an East German woman who has relatives in the Federal Republic. What did she say about her feelings in: 1949; 1952; 1961; 1970; 1972? (See **A**.)

31 The Berlin Wall

A Potsdamer Platz, Berlin, in 1932

B Potsdamer Platz in the 1960s

A and B show the same square in Berlin in 1932 and the 1960s. Why did it change? What was it like to live in Berlin after the Blockade ended? (see page 55).

The USA poured money into rebuilding West Berlin's houses, shops and factories. West Berlin became known as the 'shop window of the west'. At the same time the GDR announced that East Berlin was its capital. At first, people could move easily between East and West Berlin. Many lived in the East and worked in the West. Some left the GDR via West Berlin to live in West Germany. About 3.6 million people left GDR between 1949 and 1961, over 1.5 of them going via West Berlin.

The uprising of 17 June 1953 (see page 58) had little impact on Berlin. But in 1958 a crisis arose when Russia tried to gain control of West Berlin. On 27 November 1958 the USSR, under its leader, Khruschev, demanded that four-power control of Berlin should end.

In a note to the Federal Republic of Germany the USSR outlined the changes it wanted:

❛ . . . the Soviet Government supports the plan for giving Berlin the status of a demilitarised Free City with an independent government and administration. The Soviet Government has no intention of incorporating West Berlin into the German Democratic Republic. ❜ **(C)**

Britain, America and France rejected the demands and refused to remove their troops from West Berlin.

The Berlin Wall

A third crisis over Berlin arose in 1961 because of continuing emigration from the GDR. On 13 August 1961 the GDR built a wall to divide the Soviet from the Western sectors of Berlin (see **D**). **E** is a GDR statement on why this was done.

❛ Reliable safeguards and effective control must be insured on the West Berlin borders in order to block the way to subversive activities. ❜ **(E)**   (decree on travel restriction 12.8.61)

What was the Western response? The mayor of West Berlin, Willy Brandt, said:

❛ Not only a sort of state boundary but the wall of a concentration camp is drawn right across Berlin. The Berlin Senate protests in the face of the world against the illegal and inhuman measures taken by the partitioners of Germany, the oppressors of East Berlin and the menacers of West Berlin. ❜ **(F)**

D East German workers building the Berlin Wall

East Berliners were no longer able to visit West Berlin. Many found themselves cut off from their families or work. Some tried to escape, but barbed wire, machine guns and border guards made this hard. It became more difficult as the wall was fortified over the years. Some people made remarkable escape attempts:

❝Bowshot Flight to Freedom . . .
Two young East Berliners escaped to the West by shooting a wire rope over the Berlin Wall with the help of a bow and arrow and using a pulley to glide to freedom, it was disclosed yesterday.❞ (G)　　　(The *Daily Telegraph*, 6 April 1983)

These two were lucky. Many more died in the attempt to escape.

At Christmas 1963 West Berliners were allowed to visit their relatives in East Berlin for the first time since the building of the Berlin Wall. Similar arrangements were made throughout the 1960s, but the East Germans made it hard to carry out such visits. Improvements came in 1970 when the four powers met in Berlin.

On 3 September 1971 they signed an agreement to allow West Berliners to visit East Berlin and the GDR. This was followed by an agreement on travel to Berlin from the Federal Republic of Germany. The USSR promised to keep the routes between the Federal Republic of Germany and West Berlin open. East Germans still could not visit West Berlin or the Federal Republic.

??????????????????

1 a Describe what you can see at points **1–5** on **A** and **B**.
b Why did the Potsdamer Platz change so much between 1932 and the 1960s?

2 a What reason did the GDR give for building the Berlin Wall (**E**)? Do you think this was the real reason?
b What view did the West take of the wall (**F**)?

3 Imagine a wall is being built across the centre of your town. How will it affect your life? (Think about – going to school, shopping, seeing friends and family . . .)

4 Fill in the table below, to show how people living in the areas shown were affected by
a the building of the Berlin Wall
b the 1971/2 agreement

Area	Berlin Wall	1971/2 agreement
East Berlin GDR (outside Berlin) West Berlin FRG		

32 Two Germanies and the World

After 1949 what position did the two Germanies have in the World? Both became strong industrial powers after 1949, but they became tied to very different economic systems. The Federal Republic was tied to Western Europe and America, and the GDR to the USSR and Eastern Europe.

A shows how this happened.

The two Germanies had got some independence back after the occupation following the Second World War, but their future was decided by the two super-powers (USA and USSR).

B is an American cartoon showing the position of West Germany. C is a French cartoon showing East/West German friendship in the shadow of nuclear weapons.

A East and West German world alliances, 1950–73

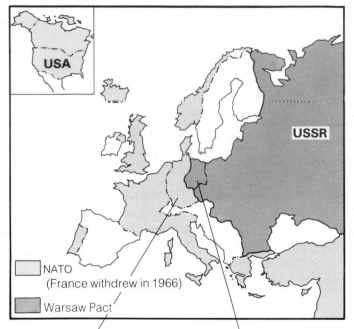

NATO
(France withdrew in 1966)

Warsaw Pact

	West Germany		East Germany
		1950	Treaty with Poland Recognised Oder-Neisse line as Polish border with Germany
1955	Could run its own affairs	**1955**	Could run its own affairs
	Joined North Atlantic Treaty Organisation (NATO)		Joined Warsaw Pact
1957	Became member of European Economic Community (EEC)		
1963	Treaty with France		
		1964	Treaty with USSR
1970	Treaty with USSR Treaty with Poland Recognised Oder- Neisse line as Polish border with Germany		
1973	Became member of United Nations (UN)	**1973**	Became member of United Nations (UN)

B West Germany is now caught up in the hostility between the 'Superpowers' – America and Russia

C Friendly relations – under the threat of nuclear arms